In Your Face IRS:
Zero Taxes

Rochit Rajsuman

Comments and questions on this book can be sent at
zerotax@justifyworld.com

In Your Face IRS: Zero Taxes

Rochit Rajsuman, Ph. D.

JustifyWorld Inc.

Library of Congress Cataloging-in-Publication Data
Rajsuman, Rochit
In Your Face IRS: Zero Taxes / Rochit Rajsuman
ISBN 9-781-4776404-5-6

© **2012 JustifyWorld Inc.**

International Standard Book Number 9-781-4776404-5-6

10 9 8 7 6 5 4 3 2 1

In Your Face IRS: Zero Taxes

Table of Contents

Disclaimer

This book contains political commentary and suggestions on life-style choices. The objective of discussion is to entertain and for provoking thought. JustifyWorld Inc. and author take no responsibility of any damages to anyone if someone tries to implement any suggestion given in this book. These discussions are generalized and do not consider specific details in anyone's life. Person considering such choices should first consult with his/her attorney, accountant and other relevant professionals, and check local, state and federal laws before taking any action.

Preface

It is customary to acknowledge the contribution of other people and express gratitude and thanks. But what should one do if pissed?

I am pissed with the congress, which gave a blank check to the Treasury on the spot and allowed Treasury officials to shift that money to a handful of people and let them do whatever they want. I am also pissed with the congress that they let bad actors go scot free. I am pissed with the Treasury and the Federal Reserve for giving over Trillion dollars of public money to few corporations. I am pissed with executives of certain banks and insurers for their bad judgment, acts and decisions that has caused suffering to millions of people.

When we pissed, we do something about it. This book is my effort to educate middle class Americans to stop funding the wasteful culture of the government. The heart and soul of a democratic nation is its people. From now on government should not waste your money; you shouldn't give your money and let it happen again.

I acknowledge the bad judgment and decision of the congress; bad decisions of the officials in the Treasury and the Federal Reserve and bad behavior of the executives on the Wall-Street, banks and insurers. Without their bad behavior, I would have never thought of writing this book.

Information is sometimes lost in a long book; hence, I have tried to keep it as short as possible and focused. I cut down a lot of entertainment from each chapter in an attempt that my base message should not be lost. A number of events, I have referred to, have been reported in the media; there is no reason for me to re-write them in this book. It will only distract readers from the objective topic I want to communicate. In today's world of Internet, interested readers can get detailed account of any event by a simple search.

My objective is to provoke thought how middle class Americans can stop the free-flow and wastage of their tax dollars – simply put, don't give tax dollars; when you don't give money, other people can't waste it. I hope after reading this book, middle class Americans will take action and eliminate their taxes; money that is being wasted by the government and given to few bad actors.

Some of my comments will appear against the Republicans, while other against the Democrats. My view is people first then animals, whether it is a donkey or an elephant.

We, the people had enough of corruption. Game is money, we will play; we will no longer stand on the sideline. We will play the game; a rigged game, and win using the same rules with an in-your-face attitude.

I know, as soon as this book is published, every minute of my life will be scrutinized and trashed in every possible way imaginable. If the rich and government officials will find a way to chastised me for speaking out, they will. I am myself saying that I paid nothing in 2010 and 2011 to the IRS as well as to the Franchise Tax Board of CA; they can audit me. I don't care who says what about me. I know who I am and what I am.

I came from poor background – my grandfather died in his youth. He wasn't rich; he was just starting out his career as a lawyer. Because of being tabooed and the stupid Indian society at the time, re-marrying was not in the lexicon for my grandmother; she had a hard life and died on street. If I am thrown out on the street, let it be; I eat beans and rise, it is healthy and doesn't cost a bit.

No, I don't have a death wish. I am a commoner, I can't fight with rich and powerful; I am gonna join them. I don't want to change my life-style; for beans and rice, I don't need to make money but that is exactly what I intend to do – make millions, become rich, rub elbow with other rich, learn their methods and tell it all.

In the past, I have told a number of my friends that both in my career and money, I have already achieved more than whatever I had imagined growing up and now I will simply enjoy. Sorry guys, I changed my mind, I need to become rich, not for my life style but to learn and educate people on the street – it is my calling.

I was advised a certain value as the list price of this book – this is fu**ing sh**, price it about $30. If I have written this book for the rich, I would have priced it over $100; all my previous books published by the Artech House Inc. are indeed priced over $100 each. Rich will also read it because it discloses their secrets. But I have written this book for the middle class America; I can't price it at $100. I would like every student, handyman, construction worker, mom-and-pop store owner, farmer, scientist, engineer, returning soldier, factory worker, and small business owner to read it and take action.

To keep the cost minimum, I didn't discuss this book with any traditional publisher. I don't use any social media website; I have looked at them and noticed blatant violation of intellectual property (IP); I will write about it in future. For the time being, because I don't use these websites, I cannot put it in your hands via these websites.

Finally, I dedicate this book to the middle class America. It was middle class that declared and fought for independence in 1776; it was middle class who built this country; it was middle class that fought world wars; it was the work of middle class that made this nation the world power; it is middle class men and women who fought the recent wars and still fighting against terrorists. My reward will be when middle class Americans will force reform and bring back the system to the state that is for the people, not for just few.

Chapter 1: Introduction

I am not talking here how mega companies shift their revenue to off-shore tax havens. I am also not talking here how billionaires pay hardly 14%-15% of their income in taxes (14%-15% is too much for me). **I am talking here how middle class America can pay zero taxes**. If you are a farmer/rancher, mom-and-pop store owner, contractor, doctor/lawyer/accountant providing services, small business owner, you should not pay a dime in taxes.

Students don't even have any earning, may be $8-$10 an hour earning from a burger place; taxes are not really an issue for them yet, but ballooning unforgivable student loan is. What I am talking here is that they need not to pay it back.

No, don't hide your income; don't break any laws. I am in-fact suggesting to follow the law to the letter. IRS can't do a sh**. IRS doesn't make laws, they follow laws. Congress makes laws. After reading this book, will congress change laws I am referring to? I challenge them, no, I dare them. If members of the congress even think to touch these laws, they will shoot in their own foot; their own assets will become venerable. Not to mention they won't get money from the rich (campaign contribution) and most likely will be voted out (or recalled) so fast that person won't be able to utter the word sorry.

Readers may be asking if there is something of this nature, why people have not used it so far. The simple fact is – people have been using it.

There are two simple and basic principles, all rich, corporations and even law makers (they are also rich), use for themselves:

1. They shift money away from their name or away from the taxable location.

2. They reduce their income on paper, for individuals it is Adjusted Gross Income (AGI).

A number of actions, I mention in this book, do fall under these two categories – shift money and reduce income; but there is lot more. You will understand it by the time you will finish chapter 5. Imagine an analogous situation – if someone finds a method to earn money without working, will that person tell it to anyone? No. The only time, you will hear about it if (a) you yourself discover it; (b) media finds out about it and report it; and (c) person is a daredevil.

What I am writing, is in-your-face proposition and can be considered under category (c). But the real reason is: I am pissed (just like the rest of the middle class). Till 2009, I paid hefty taxes each year just like any other middle class American. I am a scientist/engineer/professor or whatever you want to call me; I am sure after reading this book, some people may even use various 4-letter words. I was pissed when treasury shoved hundreds of billions in the throats of big banks and insurers.

Over Trillion dollars were siphoned-off over night, right in front of our eyes. US treasury gave hundreds of billions of dollars to corporations whether they wanted it or not. And it didn't end: because "bailout" is now a dirty word, money is given to these same mega corporations under quantitative easing (QE). Credit should not freeze; people taking mortgages should be able to get loans. Federal Reserve give money at 0% interest rate (money to banks, who else; you and I can't borrow from the Federal Reserve); 30-years mortgage rate is hovering around 4%, a net 4% to the banks. Banks get at 0% and give it to public at 4% (much much higher for car loans and credit cards). Public's tax dollars are cycled back to the public, public pay 4% (or higher) to banks and salaries/benefits/retirement of various government officials.

When we are pissed, we take action. I made changes. I paid no taxes for the year 2010 as well as for 2011. Not just federal taxes but also nothing to the Franchise Tax Board of California. Both the IRS and the Franchise Tax Board can review my tax filing and audit me.

Individual's act is small but it validates a hypothesis. Once we have proof-of-concept, we can repeat it – basic scientific principle. I would like to see that all middle class Americans eliminate their taxes – don't give money to the treasury so that they can shove it to their buddies.

There is another reason I decided to write this book. While living in the Silicon Valley, I really didn't see the impact of 2008 recession on people's life. In summer of 2010, when real estate prices were at the bottom, I purchased a condo/apartment in Las Vegas. In Vegas, I saw the impact; pictures don't show the real devastation. Neighborhood after neighborhood, rows of houses miles long, but not a soul living there. Since then, I have also seen similar situations in various parts of California. When you see the devastation with your own eyes, it is hard to remain detached. One of the richest nation on Earth and yet millions of people are literally on the street – they were thrown out on the street.

Insult to the injury – to rectify these ghost communities, government and law-makers passed few laws that in-effect let corporations and their executives, bad actors, go scot-free. In real sense, congress gave blank check and treasury shoved billions to banks giving reasons of should've, would've, could've.

It is too big; (my friends) **should** not fail. It **would** be disaster (for their personal assets); it **could** lead to depression (of bankers and insurers). We need a new law, **T**o **A**dd **R**iches and **P**rotection act, for my buddies, TARP!

Guess what, 4-years have gone, it is 2012 and still millions of people are suffering and in depression, in real depression. Rather gambling on the Wall-Street, treasury officials should drive around Vegas. After dismal job report for four straight months, February-May of 2012, pundits are talking – why after spending hundreds of billions, four years hence, job picture is not improving? Are these people pundits or idiots? Hundreds of billions were not spent to create jobs. Treasury shoved billions of dollars to bank executives; these bank executives still have their cushy jobs, they have no complain. Shouldn't government official be prosecuted for the misuse of public funds?

If these bank and corporations like AIG were nationalized that **should've** brought public confidence in government; it **would've** removed bad actors and **could've** been a real reform.

Because only reform was done was to reward banks, these banks went back to the same risky practices. In May 2012, JP Morgan Chase lost billions in the same hedging and trading of the same derivatives. Company took action and forced a number of executives out – hefty retirement packages and scot free from any liability, wasn't it used to be called golden parachute! When the story broke, in an interview on MSNBC, New York Governor Spitzer called Financial Service Committee "bunch of jokers". No, Mr. Spitzer, it is conflict of interest; it's lobbying money, campaign contribution. Their act is deliberate, congress can't make laws and regulators can't regulate their benefactors. Laws have already been made to get unrestricted donations; you can challenge, even the Supreme Court can't do anything, Supreme Court can only follow the laws. Public can't do a thing, system is rigged to the core.

When someone proposes a regulation or reform, i.e. Mr. Volker, congress performs its duty of checks and balance: check if there are enough loopholes, balance it for the benefit of lobbyists.

When someone asks about bailout of automakers, the same politicians answer that they should have gone through Chapter-11 bankruptcy protection and subsequent re-structuring. Have you ever heard a single word of this nature for these banks and insurers? No, do you know why? Automakers employ thousands of middle class Americans, banks don't. Rich and well connected, yet, CEO of GM did lose his job because he flew to Washington in a private jet and rubbed it in their faces; bank CEOs didn't do any such stupidity. You don't rub face of your buddy in the dirt. Bank CEOs didn't even get a slap on the hand. Let another thousand of auto workers, middle class Americans lose their jobs, homes and livelihood; they are common people not the members of our club!

Just a few years ago, Arthur Anderson debacle sent shock waves worldwide and created real confidence crisis. Not bailing out took the bad actors out permanently. Did it lead to disaster? Yeah, for the executives of Arthur Anderson and few other corporations who were cooking books.

Government will treat everyone the same – on the Mars may be. Former competitor, Lehman Brothers went under bally, no problem. Its in-fact very good, competition is gone and now, we also got an example to spin that we didn't bail them out.

Another argument was given on credit freeze. When banks are nationalized and the same Trillion dollars are available, the word credit freeze doesn't even appear in the lexicon; even the combined GDP of the so called PIGS countries is not trillion dollars. Nationalization of-course means plummeting stock prices of these banks and insurers, wiping out billion of personal assets of these executive. That was the real problem, if corporations are nationalized, the rich executives go bankrupt.

Nationalization of banks would also mean avoiding foreclosure of millions of homes and harm to the public as it has been. Jobs of common people were lost. Nationalization doesn't cause job loss for common people, people become government employees; it does cause job loss for the executives.

Events were too fast. FDIC has taken over local failed banks overnight. Federal employees were already in these banks going over their books; Treasury and Federal Reserve had whole weekend.

Oh yeah, the congressional hearing of the bank executives; what was the purpose – to grill them or to tell them that they are scot-free from that day onwards. What an incredible and belligerent insult to the intelligence of public. Hey, give me hundreds of billion and feel free to say anything verbally; not just one time, anytime; I won't object, may even accept being greedy, unethical and immoral; no fifth, no nothing.

After the crash of 1929 and depression of 1930s, billions were not shoved to the rich. The handful of people who were spiking stock prices in late 1920s became bankrupt. But this time, the handful of bad actors responsible for spiking real-estate/mortgages/derivatives not only went scot free, they also got additional billions in their pockets.

In 1930s, instead of shoving billions to few, projects like Golden Gate Bridge and Hoover dam were funded to create jobs and the very same "depressed" people created world icons. American workers took the stage and became admiration and envy of the world. Can you mention a single such project this time? This time around, even developing and third world countries are questioning American authority. People don't have work, they can't show what they are capable of, so work/ingenuity is no longer the envy of the world, money is.

Both rich and lawmakers say that in 1929, stock market was un-regulated, today, there are regulations. Really! Regulations for whom, for the common public or for the rich? Whether individual rich people (Angel Investors), venture capitalists (VCs) or investment banks, they buy company stock in pennies when public hasn't even heard the company. There are no regulations; transaction value and number of shares are based upon negotiation between the company's founders and investors. After such initial sale, stock price is spiked. Underwriter bank put a value for IPO – there is a calculation, don't be fool by that math. I can't go through it here, but in Internet age, information is available, look it up. It's is arbitrary. The words "estimate" and "projection" themselves, by definition have nothing concrete, numbers pull out of a hat. When company becomes public and public buy, they sell – pump & dump, pure and simple.

Founders of Ford, Microsoft, Cisco, Google and many other companies rightfully deserve billions; they never asked public money, they need not to. If an insurer issues a policy/contract without ever having ability to pay for the contract, that is equivalent to a con job. Instead putting in jail, giving billions of dollars is flat-out corruption by the government official in-charge; they should be indicted for corruption and prosecuted.

"Too big corporation" by existing laws must be broken down so that corporation cannot exert undesired influence and jeopardizes nations and public welfare. This is the reason Standard Oil was broken down and anti-trust laws were made. These laws are still on the book. With these banks and insurers, congress did not follow them and still not following them, no one even talk about it. Legislative responsibility is checks and balance; phrase often used by the same law makers who gave blank check to the treasury on the spot when treasury officials told them of potential failure of big banks –

where is the due diligence?

Without due diligence, allowing treasury to give over Trillion dollars of public money on the spot, for "too big" corporations; public may consider it as government's negligence but public cannot do anything. A constitution scholar might know if there is a process through which public can charge government officials, unfortunately, I am not aware of any such process. Law makers have made solid laws for their own protection, didn't they?

They did pass a law to reform Wall Street – member of congress now cannot trade on the insider's information, till now, they were above the law.

Is congress still sleeping? Mortgage based derivatives are now known, is anyone checking commodity based derivative, no not traditional options, secondary/tertiary derivatives and the type of derivatives that were created using mortgages? Is anyone checking the so called secondary market where companies are selling stocks to public without any regulations, requirements and restrictions? These are legitimate questions one would like to know the answers of.

No, the first question, I would like to know is how much campaign contribution these banks and executives gave and to whom in 2010 election and how much they are giving now? I don't have resource to investigate and compile this data. I am a bit surprise that media didn't report this data; journalists should investigate and report it.

Voting them out may be some consolation. In-fact, there should be law of maximum 2-terms, but who's going to pass such a law? Law makers cannot, it is straight conflict of interest.

Silicon Valley hi-tech companies have an unwritten policy – restructure every two year and change job responsibilities of majority of people including engineers, scientists, engineering managers and even VPs. Regardless of their job performance, they are re-assigned to different job. Over past 50 years,

Silicon Valley has shown that "don't disturb an employee if he/she is doing good job" is hogwash. When employees are periodically disturbed, they infact do a better job. This restructuring is not a layoff but it does cleanout dead wood by attrition. It keeps employees honest, productive and forces them to learn new things.

Members of congress are employees of public, not the ruler as they behave. If you vote them out and replace them regardless of what they did in the elected term, newly elected person is likely to be more tuned to the constituents and will have less money-connections. Subsequently, less conflict of interest. And before he/she gets comfortable, replace him/her. When big corporations, big money will learn that the person won't be re-elected, they are likely to pay less or nothing in the campaign contribution; lobbying shrinks. Get it clear in your mind America – when you vote for a "powerful" member of the congress or state assembly, thinking that person will get federal/state funding for your local cause, you are promoting corruption. In a clean democracy, there should be no "powerful" elected official. Person becomes "powerful" when he/she remains in the system for too long and thus, gets the "power" to bend the system according to personal wishes; like Putin. This is why constitution has term-limit for the President; it is unfortunate that it doesn't have term limit for the congress.

One time voting out is one time replacement process; another politician will take the job that may be as bad if not worse from the beginning. In the absence of term-limit, fundamental problem is that too much money is in the system. It's an age old saying – too much money brings corruption. At-least take your money out. You, the middle class America needs to make changes – don't give your money, taxes, for them to control.

You give one-third of your income in taxes to the treasury; treasury shove it to mega corporations right in front of your eyes; mega corporations give millions to law makers in the name of campaign contribution, openly; law makers make laws for their own exuberant salaries/benefits/retirement and for the protection of bankers and insurers, again publicly; government siphons more of your money. The cycle continues.

What can you do – chock the pipeline. Eliminate your taxes by using the laws that they dare not touch. If they want cycle to continue, it won't be your money. Although, unimaginable, if they do change the laws, we get a plain field.

All over the country, people are protesting against banks and mega corporations, so called occupy movement. But don't you see, the complaint of occupiers is against the morality and ethics of banks/corporations, that's nuts. Do you really think you can affect the morality/ethics of any corporation? If they protest in-front of law-makers, they might be more effective because law-makers need votes. Bank/corporations don't give a damn to any occupier; besides ethics and morality have no meaning for them. If there is an illegal act, government might slap on the hand, put a token fine and get them off the hook. Multi-billion dollar company being fined in couple of millions, who are they kidding? Couple of millions are not even enough for the party these executive hold.

Everything is rigged to the extent that I believe it is un-repairable. A rigged game of Chess. The only thing you can do is learn the rules of the game and play. It is rigged; they can change laws, the rules of the game in the middle of the game. Hence, use the laws that they cannot change; laws, if changed, would leave their king in the open and subjected to check. Now, we can play and beat them in their own game.

Since the purchase of condo/apartment, I had option to skip California taxes by declaring Las Vegas as my residence, like Apple did according to NY Times story in April-2012 or what many rich do. I didn't change my residence. I didn't need to when I can bring my Adjusted Gross Income (AGI) to a sufficiently low level. Eventually, I will declare

Vegas as my home; it is the easiest thing and lot less paper work. There are some additional advantages – free boos everywhere. I am not drinking but making spelling mistakes! Don't be confused; Vegas girls are professional.

Whether it is county, state or federal law makers, while quoting statistics, politician emphasize that majority of tax revenue comes from the rich. Let the treasury live on this so called "majority tax revenue".

We, the people had enough. We will use the same laws, follow them to the letter and pay no more. Legislators serve the rich; go get your revenue from the rich – all of it. If rich pay 15% in taxes, middle class Americans should pay zero.

Game on, they want to play, let's play.

Elevator talk, in one line – get your Adjusted Gross Income (AGI) under the poverty line. You can even bring your AGI to almost zero but there is no need for that. Don't call yourself middle class, call yourself poor. Forget taxes, you are now qualified for food stamps. Really! It's up to you, although, I don't recommend; it will make hard life of poor harder. Leave food stamps etc. for the people who need such help; eliminate your taxes and sleep soundly with good conscious.

Because of the bragging culture, some people may have psychological difficulty in calling themselves poor, word poor is tabooed. Don't brag, bragging is a cardinal sin; it is hurting you. Didn't Jesus ask to be meek in Beatitudes? Poor people don't have anything; if you don't earn money, why should you pay taxes? Besides, it is just a word. If you know yourself, what difference does it make on the use of word to describe you? 10-20 years ago, words geek and nerd were tabooed; now, they are in fashion, everyone wants to be a nerd.

How can you bring your AGI under the poverty line, will take few chapters; that's why it is a book and not a magazine article. I have tried to compile a set of "rules" at the end. This book is not a murder mystery, but I still recommend that reader go through the whole text. Reading the whole text will help in understanding of the underlying reasoning and to determine what actions to take according to the person's own specific conditions.

I can give you couple of quick examples. I made a mistake that I didn't eliminate/reduce Santa Clara County's property taxes for my home. We learn from mistakes. Now, the only thing I can do is to sell it!

Example 1: By selling home at a fractional value, new assessed value and taxes can be reduced; these values will be based upon the new purchased amount – new purchased amount becomes the assessed value and no one can contradict it. I learned this method of house transaction from my own neighborhood. Sell your home to your kids or parents. If you don't want to do that, establish a trust and sell it to the trust. Don't sell it for $1; you won't be able to fight the county's assessor office. Use a decent value. If you can find a licensed assessor, get a new home assessment. You can use it to challenge the county's assessed value. You don't have to go through selling process and the cost associated with it. Assessment is an opinion anyway. In 2005-2007, home assessment values were spiked-up at the direction of lenders (to write bigger loans and bigger commission); now try if you can spike them down. There are no standards; government won't set-up a standard. Talk about conflict of interest, in 2005-2007, government turned a blind eye because it allowed them to siphon more of your money. If you are able to spike-down the value, they won't turn a blind eye; they will be all over you because it reduces their revenue, your taxes. Get the right paper work otherwise, you can't play the game.

If you are planning to move, then don't "sell"; just get a desired assessment. In moving situation, your objective should be tax-free gain of up to $250,000 (for couples). Don't do anything that might adversely affect this tax-free gain.

□ □ □

Example 2: Lets look another example that many readers may feel more familiar – Roth IRA (Individual Retirement Account). All assets in Roth IRA are tax exempt, not only the original contribution but also all income. There are also other advantages in terms of accessibility, no minimum distribution requirements and passing to heirs (interested readers should look it up). Hence, everyone recommends contributing in Roth IRA; money is protected from taxes. People who lost their jobs, many are still losing and can't find new job; they don't have money to contribute in the Roth IRA (if you do, good). But while you are unemployed, shift your assets into tax exempt account. First, transfer all your retirement contribution accumulated in 401K/403b into an IRA. Also, open a Roth IRA and transfer $20,000-$25,000 from your IRA to Roth IRA before December 31st; it is called Roth Conversion. A cautionary remark: use trustee-to-trustee transfer for 401K/403b conversion into an IRA as well as from IRA to Roth IRA conversion; it will keep your life simple. By January 31st, you will receive all income statements, mortgage statement etc. You will also receive Form 1099-R and Form 5498, identifying Roth conversion amount.

In February, prepare your taxes, not for filing but for estimation. Roth conversion amount is money taken out from IRA and hence subjected to taxes. You are unemployed, so this is your income. Because you may have some other income, as well as deductions like mortgage interests and property taxes, the initial calculation might show that you owe federal and state taxes. In tax preparation software, play with Roth conversion amount and find the exact amount that if converted into Roth would render zero taxes. For argument sake, let's say, it is $18,000. But let's say, you had converted $25,000 and hence, it is $7000 that is causing you to owe federal and state taxes. Well, un-convert these $7000; it is called re-characterization. You must do re-characterization before April 15, before filing your taxes. Essentially, you have $18,000 converted from IRA to Roth IRA. IRS considers it as your income, let them, you are at the poverty line and not paying any taxes. Money was in your 401K/403b, first it got transferred into an IRA and now it is in Roth IRA. You never paid a dime in taxes on this money and now, this amount is tax protected forever. You can invest it any which way you like, income or gains are also tax protected.

□ □ □

Seriously, I am not kidding, I didn't invent anything written in this book. I learned and still learning, you should too.

People who have jobs and small business owners who have business and other income can't do Roth conversion of this nature, or at-most may be able to convert just a token amount. Reduction of property taxes can also be within $1000-$2000 range, or just a token amount. So, essentially both of these examples are peanuts. Let's eliminate all of your income from taxes. Let's bring your AGI under the poverty line and make you poor and broke. When you are poor, you don't owe any taxes; you would need food stamps and welfare!

Before I get to the meat, keep in mind that America is an English language country. Choose the right words, i.e., are you middle class or poor. Bad choice of word is bad for you. For example, many Asian and African countries are not English speaking nations; those people are not proficient in English. They use words like bribery. If you use such poor English, indeed, you should be punished for not learning the language (of the business). Use decent word, like lobbying. You will not only be alright, members of congress will in-fact rub elbow with you. Behavior should also be classy. Never ever give lobbying money to a law-maker; royals don't handle trivial things themselves. Thousand years ago, even knights had counts and squires to handle such trivial things like money. Even the nutcase Don Quixote had good squire Sancho Panza to keep the wallet and to carry out all financial transactions. Whenever it is hard cold cash, give it to staff, they handle campaign contribution.

Chapter 2: Designation and Structure of a Corporation

Because my proposition is for the middle class America, farmers and ranchers, mom-and-pop store owners, present and would be small business owners, and students; it is fair to assume that some readers may not know the types of corporations (designation) and their structure. Let me review it very briefly in few paragraphs and then I will get back to our main topic.

Each business has to operate under certain laws that include city, state and federal laws. If you are starting a business, it is not necessary to consult an attorney from day-one. But one should try to familiarize with basic city and state laws. Most City-Hall and chamber of commerce provide extensive information on various laws, regulations as well as on various government agencies. Most states have Department that issues business licenses; most regulatory forms are available from the Department of Corporation (Business, Commerce). Internal Revenue Service (IRS) web-site and Small Business Administration web-site also have necessary links and a wealth of information for small business owners.

The Sole Proprietorship, Limited Liability Corporation (LLC) and "C" Corporation are few commonly used designations of a company. Other designations are Limited Partnership and "S" Corporation; these have fallen out of favor because of no protection against liability claims and business debt. Each designation has different tax and liability consequences. "C" Corporation provides the best protection among these designations.

Sole Proprietorship is the worst designation. Not just from tax point of view, it also doesn't provide any liability protection to the business owner. Yet most small business owners start their business as sole proprietorship. There are more than 8-million sole proprietorship small businesses in the United States.

These are all sitting on a live and ticking time bomb. A single mishap can not only bankrupt the business but also the business owner. Indeed, examples can be seen in just about every town when the business and business owner end-up bankrupt because of the liability law-suit. Small business owner should not use Sole Proprietorship, it is suicidal.

Sole proprietorship has its use and if properly used it can provide some very desirable advantages to the founder of the business, particularly when business is based upon a new technology, new concept. That discussion is beyond the scope of this book.

Because of the personal protection to the business owner, regardless of the type of business, for a mom-and-pop shop, I recommend "C" Corporation among the above mentioned designations. Reasons are:

1. C Corporation is an independent entity with its own tax id (employer identification number, EIN). Thus, it requires a separate tax filing. But being an independent entity it is

separate from the entrepreneur's personal assets. Hence, if a liability or debt claim occurs against the company, business owner's personal assets are not affected. Sole Proprietorship doesn't make such distinction and hence, owner's personal assets can be claimed in a liability suit. In the American litigation society, it is pertinent and prudent to safe-guard against personal lawsuit.

2. The corporate tax rate is lower for C Corporation in comparison to the tax rate a person is subjected to if the equivalent income is obtained from sole proprietorship. However, when corporate income is passed to the owner such as salary, the amount is taxed as personal income. To avoid this and to maintain lower tax rate, I suggest, business owner to draw only a small salary as personal income and use left-over corporate income to grow the business. Salary is an operating expense to the business, it is no longer

income to the business and hence, business doesn't pay tax on it. By controlling the salary, owner can maintain personal income to remain in the 25% tax bracket; why not move to 15% or even zero! It should be noted that if desired, owner can transfer any/all income to himself/herself at anytime. In this context, bonus and/or dividend pay-off are simple means to transfer the income from the business to the business owner. Sole Proprietorship doesn't allow such control.

3. If business is sold, person effectively sells stock that has been held for long time. Hence, long-term capital gain tax is applicable; a substantially lower tax-rate.

4. Business owner can transfer business to heirs without taxation by assigning them the officers of the corporation (more on this later in this chapter).

However, I should point-out that person should keep his/her personal finances completely separate and with proper documentation – a full paper trail. For example, person should not write a personal check for the business. If he/she writes a personal check, than have it reimbursed from the business. Similarly, the initial capital the founder put-in should be structured as a loan to the business with a promissory note from the company.

C Corporation designation also requires some formalities, i.e., meeting of the board of directors and annual shareholder meeting. For small business, with single director, these formalities can be fulfilled at any time. All that is needed for these formalities is a binder that maintains date and minutes of the meeting. For example, board of directors meeting can be done when person is sitting on a toilet bowl! Yeah, laws and regulations are sh**. The Wall Street calls it "executive talent" that deserves millions in compensation. Indeed, it is a talent; not many people can sh** like this.

A separate bank account, separate tax filing and certain formalities add paper work and book keeping but it provides tremendous tax advantage and personal safety to the business owner. I should re-emphasize that when personal finances are mixed-up, or formalities are skipped, personal protection becomes questionable. A liability claimant may provide proof of personal finances in the business dealings and convince court to "pierce the veil", thus striping the personal protection of the C corporation.

Essentially, I am suggesting that all business owners establish a company, a C Corporation, and become its CEO; an employee even if it is a small business. A number of people suggest Limited Liability Corporation (LLC) for small businesses. I disagree with such conventional wisdom. One should recognize that as soon as business is funded, C Corporation issues stock, the ownership of C Corporation becomes shared. In essence, it becomes a partnership with all protections and provisions intact. When it is founder's own money (I suggested to structure it as a loan), and founder becomes an employee then effectively it becomes a partnership between founder the financier, and founder the employee. Such benefits are not available in any other structure. LLC structure is better than sole proprietorship but C Corporation provide the maximum flexibility, protection and venue for various strategies.

There is also a question of how to maintain control over the business. The capital structure of C Corporation is authorized number of shares and the par value of each share. This number is declared in the article of incorporation filed at the office of the secretary of the state. If it is a small business, i.e., a store or a deli, founder/owner can issue all shares to himself/herself. However, I suggest leaving most shares in the company (more on this later). If there are multiple share holders, than issue 51% shares to him/hers and leave rest in the company for future use. With proper clause in the company by-laws, 51% share holder can maintain control over the enterprise (more on this later).

Leaving large number of shares in company's name provide additional benefits. Primary benefit being that these cannot be taken away from the person – if you don't own something, it cannot be taken away form you! Once again, it should be realized that if desired, small business owner can issue (or purchase) these shares at any time.

The Articles of Incorporation and stock certificate requires following information:

א א א

1. Name of business
2. Duration of company (often perpetual is used)
3. Purpose of the company (what product or services)
4. Authorized shares and par value of each share
5. Initial capitalization
6. Address of the corporation and name/address of the registered agent
7. Number of directors with names and addresses

8. Name and address of incorporator (person filling the form)
9. A clause limiting liability of directors can be listed from the beginning

א א א

The securities represented by this certificate have not been registered under the securities act of 1933 (the "Act"), as amended or registered or qualified under any state securities laws. The securities must not be sold or offered for sale or otherwise distributed unless the securities are registered under the Act or an exemption there is available.

The shares represented by this certificate are subjected to a right of first refusal option in favor of the Corporation and /or it assignee(s), as provided in the bylaws of the Corporation."

"For value receive ___ hereby sell, assign and transfer unto _____ shares represented by the within certificate, and do hereby irrevocably constitute and appoints _____ attorney to transfer the said shares on the books of the within named corporation with full power of substitution in the premises.

א א א

A person can easily create an official looking certificate by a variety of software programs available in the market. For all practical purposes, it doesn't have to be official looking certificate. The same language on a simple piece of paper (a simple text document) is adequate. The corporation and stock buyer should also have a stock purchase agreement. To establish this purchase and the base value, person should also send a letter to the IRS. The letter maintains a record for the future sale. The example language is as follows:

א א א

Director of Internal Revenue
         Date
Internal Revenue Service Center

RE: Election under Section 83(b)

This statement constitutes an election pursuant to Section 83(b) of the Internal Revenue Code of 1986, as amended from time to time.

Pursuant to Treasury Regulation Section 1.83-2, the following information is submitted:

1. Name   Address
   Social Security No.
2. Property Description: n number of share of xyz Corporation.
3. Date on which property was transferred

4. The taxable year for which election is made
5. Restriction: (Such as Corporation shall have option to repurchase)
6. Fair Market Value: (The fair market value at the time of transfer of the property with respect to which this election is made, determined without regard to any restriction other than a restriction which by its terms will never lapse, is one cent, $0.01).
7. The amount paid by the undersigned taxpayer for the property is nX$0.01
8. A copy of the statement has been furnished to xyz Corporation and the transferee of the property if different from the purchaser

Sincerely,

(Signature)

א א א

I mentioned a benefit in terms of passing business to heirs without triggering taxes. The same principle is also applicable in bringing a new partner without requiring a change in structure and avoiding adverse effect in case of a family dispute. Consider a family dispute arising from a contested divorce. In communal property states, a contested divorce is almost a guarantee to destroy the business if it is a sole proprietorship. Breaking of personal relation is hard enough, should the person also loose his/her livelihood? If the business is a C Corporation, then divorcing spouse is entitled to only half of what the CEO own. If CEO owns 10% then spouse gets 5% shares and business can continue. When company has large number of shares, these can be issued to the CEO bringing CEO's stack back to whatever is desired. Furthermore, company can issue more shares and thus diluting the percentage of divorcing spouse. Stock split and reverse-split are common practices to dilute or strengthen the shares.

In above paragraphs, I mentioned a phrase – proper clause in the company by-laws. It is highly recommended that soon after the company is registered, business owner set-up basic company by-laws to cement the personal protection obtained by C Corporation. Common templates of corporation by-laws are available from various government agencies, sometimes also from the Chamber of

Commerce, from most law-firms dealing with corporate laws and even some software programs that are sold in the electronic mega-stores. While most clauses in these templates would seem trivial, an important protection clause can be established against personal law-suit.

Another clause to include in the company by-laws is on voting rights. At many companies, founder can be voted-out by the board of directors or by the shareholder's vote. By maintaining majority shares, founder can control; only he/she can vote himself/herself out. When company maintains a large number of shares (as I suggested above); the by-laws should contain a clause specifying voting right of such shares. In such case, it can be founder or the Chairman of the board or whatever title business owner has chosen for him/her. In case of small businesses when founder is the only director, by-laws can specify decision either by the director or by the majority share holder.

Founders of Google, Facebook and Zynga have demonstrated that through company by-laws, founders of public company can maintain full control on the company by maintaining voting rights. In such model, the board and share holders have essentially no saying in the operation and governance of the company. In C Corporation, when additional capital is needed, business owner should consider selling a class of shares with no voting rights, class B share.

Some additional notes on protection, before we look into how to structure income and expenses. First, what every estate planning attorney tells to individuals. Establish a signature authority, who can or cannot sign on behalf of the company. Power of attorney should be part of this planning in case of an accident, who can sign on behalf of the founder/CEO.

Similar to the company's by-laws, an employee handbook should be prepared. This can wait but should be done as soon as company starts hiring.

Once again, owner should remember that the objective is self-protection in case of a misappropriation by an employee or personal conflict between two employees. An attorney can help here without any specific instructions; most corporate attorneys can give a boiler-plate employee handbook at a very short notice. Small business owners can also use ready-made templates (from books and software) that include common rules of conduct and policies for employees. In the beginning, such templates are adequate. As company grows, additional provisions can be added.

Finally, person should evaluate operational and business dependencies and take every step to minimize or eliminate them. There should be contingency plan for business operation to continue independently regardless of an employee, a contractor, a supplier and/or a service provider. Business owner should evaluate "if an employee/contractor is run-over by a truck, who can continue his/her work without a set-back". Such planning also helps in maintaining the cost of contractor/supplier; if contractor/supplier increases charges, person can switch-over to the contingent contractor/supplier maintaining the business without sever impact.

People doing jobs should realize that this is why they need to re-think of their own welfare, work and career. A smart business man or a company will not become dependent on anyone. In other words, no employee will be critical. Any employee can be replaced or even eliminated at any time. If a person wants job security, then that person needs to become employee in his/her own business.

Operating Expenses

There are few magical words and phrases in the English language; Operating Expenses is one of them.

In the previous section, I mentioned that all businesses should register themselves as C Corporations. Business owner should become an employee, its CEO/President. As an employee, CEO should draw a small salary, preferably close to poverty-line. The surplus income should be left in the company. With minimum salary, person can control his/her personal income taxes to a lower tax bracket (target zero). The surplus amount left in the company is also not subjected to FICA taxes as it would be if person takes it in, in a higher salary.

With only a small salary, person cannot buy much; indeed, they should not buy anything from their personal income. The most of the salary will go into savings (more on it later). Whatever is needed for livelihood, let the company (C Corporation) buy it for its key employee! Let's look at what the rich do:

Consider lunch/dinner, if business can afford it, CEO can eat at any restaurant no matter how expensive and order any Italian or French wine. Have a meeting with someone and it is a business meeting paid by the company. For company, it is an operating expense. All that is needed for the IRS is a receipt and a note on who met with the CEO; but it is a legal business expense. Consider lunch with your friend CEO to discuss business strategies or future dealings – *selection of restaurant for lunch on next Friday*. Of-course, one meeting is not enough. The friend CEO will pick the tab of the second meeting and have it reimbursed as a business expense from his/her company. Am I forgetting IRS per diem regulation; no, that is designed for the poor sole-proprietors to encourage eating hamburgers and to keep them healthy.

Ever wondered how a real estate agent, who hardly makes any sale, drives around in a Mercedes? Or ever felt tired of paying auto insurance. Forget about puny insurance, company can buy or lease a new car for the use of its employees. Mercedes and BMW are for the common folks, think-of Rolls or Austin Martin. When company's key employee, the CEO, goes somewhere, it should provide a good image of the company. Now, you don't own a car, you don't pay for the insurance. Its company's car, company will pay for its insurance, just as it will pay for the gasoline; all operating expenses. Rich don't bother with $0.25/mile tax deduction; they know IRS has great sense of humor. While at-it, don't feel envious of other CEOs. If company can afford it, company can buy a Learjet or Gulfstream for its employees. Of-course, CEO's time is more important, so most of the time it will be busy flying CEO than anyone else (don't rub it in the faces of law-makers).

Ever worried about the home mortgage? Don't own a home – no home, no mortgage. Company has surplus cash that needs to be invested. Real estate is pretty good investment – company should buy a mansion with swimming pool, tennis court and servant quarters (company has to hire someone for up keeping of its investment). Keeping an empty house is not a good idea, so company should rent it out. Wait, doesn't that self-proprietary company, I was talking about, needs a place. The rent is of-course an operating expense for the self-proprietary company. We don't want readers to get too excited, but if company can afford it, company can also get an apartment on the Fifth Avenue in Manhattan overlooking the Central Park because our CEO has lunch-meetings with the Wall-Street investors on regular basis. And to decorate this apartment, company needs to buy couple of original Monet and Picasso.

Its middle of February, everyone is fed-up with snow. Isn't a conference being held in Aruba on …; oh, does it matter on what. Company would want to send its CEO to check what the conference is all about. If company has not purchased a jet (yet), CEO would need a chartered plane. Family just tags along on an empty plane, just as they crashed in the CEO's suite at the Ritz.

Girl friend wants a new dress. Company can hire her and provide a necklace (diamonds) along with the dress for …. Well, consultant to improve the moral of executive employee may be too much for some readers; how about model for the advertising campaign. Just make sure her picture appears somewhere, such as on an obscure section of the company's web-site in case IRS started to get tipsy. By the way, did I mention that our CEO can also appear in the ad in a three-piece Armani suit personalized tailored in Milan, paid by the company.

Birthday of spouse, have a Roman party on Las Vegas strip; just invite few employees and directors and it is off-site meeting to determine strategic direction of the company. Companies often have such million dollar meetings in Las Vegas, even federal agencies; everything operating expenses.

And don't forget, operating expenses are pre-tax dollars; that itself is a considerable advantage.

Transfer everything to company, don't convert business profits into higher salary or personal income – if there is no personal income, there are no personal taxes. Take $1.00 in annual salary and establish yourself as an altruist. A number of CEOs of large companies do that routinely. It's a very good PR. The real money resides with millions of shares that are collected as stock option grant. Of-course, with $1.00 annual salary you can forget taxes; in-fact, if you wish, you can apply for food stamps. Car, home, airplane, yacht are all company assets for its employees, CEO is just an employee. Lunch, dinner, trips (don't use the word "vacation") are all necessary business expenses. Who said to conduct work-meeting over a Subway sandwich. Company has surplus cash, why not eat at the Four Seasons (on any day of the week, one can see Wall-Street power brokers at Four Seasons in New York); and while waiting for the table, take a bottle of '63 Don

Perignon with Beluga caviar – it may taste like horse sh** (manure), but we are not talking taste here.

I hope readers got the point. There is nothing illegal here, it's a private company and its director(s) can choose how company is run, spend or invest its income. Although, I have written above examples light heartedly; these examples are not far from reality. CEOs and executive of all large companies routinely have such operating expenses. Some celebrities do the same with charitable Trust. Because details are "confidential", nobody can question where exactly money is going. As long as money doesn't go to personal account, IRS can't do a thing.

Not drawing salary and structuring of compensation in certain manner is what makes billionaires pay fewer taxes than their secretaries! What is stopping small business owners to not use the same methods – sole proprietorship.

I only mentioned lavish expenses and day-to-day life; ever wonder how the life-style of rich people is never affected even when they accrued large personal debt or when they lose big personal liability suit. Transfer everything to an entity, a Trust and become its trustee. Don't own anything and go broke on paper. If person is broke, creditor cannot collect anything. Being an independent entity, Trust, on the other hand can spend anything, anytime, in any manner according to the direction of trustee without being affected by the claimant (more in chapter 5). Married people beware, unless you set-up a proper multi-layered structure, spousal assets can be claimed.

Back to the surplus income small business CEO will leave in the company, it can be transferred to the person via a number of methods such as dividend, retirement contribution and other deferred compensation mechanisms. Contribution into 401K is the simplest process. It is an employee benefit, an operating expense to the company; company doesn't pay taxes on an expense. But because it is a deferred income to our CEO, CEO doesn't pay taxes either. Furthermore, because person is receiving a small salary, person will be qualified to contribute maximum into a Roth IRA that can grow without taxation and minimum distribution requirement. This is where our CEO spends his/her minimum salary that keeps him close to the poverty-line on paper.

Consider our small business CEO is a 60 year old person. Close to retirement and hence, according to the conventional wisdom not a good candidate for the Roth IRA. But let's say our CEO does set-up a Roth IRA and fund it from his small salary that we suggested should go into savings. On this Roth IRA, our CEO declares his/her 2-years old grand child as beneficiary. Now, the whole amount of Roth IRA is transferred to this grand child (heir), after his/her demise. The distribution time-frame is also now according to the kid's life expectancy, allowing the amount to continually grow without taxation. Our small business CEO may not be a millionaire, but the grand kid definitely will be and kid won't pay any taxes on this amount either.

Earlier, I mentioned that the business can be passed-on to heirs without taxation. With C Corporation, this transfer is simply to assign heirs as the officer of the corporation, i.e., son/daughter can become the next CEO and director. Founder CEO was an employee, he is retiring. Corporation hires a new CEO; it just happens that the new CEO is the son/daughter of the old CEO. As company has majority of shares with voting rights are limited to the founder/CEO, founder/CEO doesn't pass-on large number of shares or estate to his/her heirs. Nonetheless, heir when become the CEO, gets the voting rights and the full control; he/she can run the company in any which way desired. Any time in future, if they want, they can issue these shares to themselves; I recommend "a purchase". If no estate is passed-on, there are no taxes. Who cares about "death taxes"; let congress tinker any which way they want, they need something to keep busy anyway.

While mentioning death, we also want to protect the family of our CEO. From the surplus that was left in the company by not taking large salary, company can buy life insurance for the CEO; another operating expense. Because our CEO is very important person, company can buy few million dollars policy. If something happens to our CEO, beneficiary gets the policy's amount without taxation.

So, what is the cardinal law for small businesses and farmers and ranchers in the American heartland? By now, it should be clear – ditch Self-proprietorship, it Sucks; move to Cash-Cow, the C Corporation. Ranch and farm owners should stop calling themselves ranchers and farmers. They should become CEOs of companies engaged in agriculture or food business. Draw a small salary and if operating expenses cause company to run in loss, increase food prices. If someone asks, show the loss figures; if congress doesn't like higher prices, they can provide subsidy, similar to big oil companies!

This is what large companies do – On March 24, 2011, the New York Times reported that for 2010 General Electric reported worldwide profit of $14.2B; $5.1B from the United States. It paid no taxes and in-fact claimed tax benefits of $3.2B. The CEOs of other companies need to re-calibrate their thinking. 2-3 millions may be enough for a party but it is not serious money unless someone throws a billion here and a billion there!

Let's consider one more example before moving to the next aspect. Above, I mentioned that small business owner should leave a large number of shares in the company for future use, i.e., to bring a partner. But let's say our CEO wants to sell the company and 51% shares are in his/her name. One possibility is that our CEO value the whole company to his/her 51% shares and sell, thus, get the total value. But if planned ahead, our CEO can buy leftover 49% shares at a much higher price. It is a non-public company, investor and company can "negotiate" any price. Our small business CEO continues running the company for a year. During this year, company can contribute its cash (including the cash from the stock sale) in dividend payment and to the retirement of our CEO. Then the sale occurs, 100% shares owned by the CEO, 49% shares were held over a year; hence, person will be subjected to long-term capital gain tax. The original 51% share will create large capital gain (par value was very small when company was registered). But the 49% shares can cause a significant long-term capital loss, offsetting the total tax bill.

If majority shares were in the company, the sale of company can be adjusted to cause net long-term as well as short-term capital loss; offsetting gains and income from other sources.

Such sales happen all the time with added manipulation in the number of shares. When third party own some stock, by proper splitting, reverse-splitting, new issue and by using buyer's stock, most of the value is transferred to founder/CEO at the lowest tax rate. Third party, including the tax-man, gets nothing, at-best few peanuts. Individual small stores, restaurants, ranches and farms can also be bought and sold in this manner if it is a C Corporation.

It is worth mentioning here that what I am suggesting is not new; the only new aspect is that I am suggesting it for all businesses including small businesses, mom-and-pop stores, and even ranches and farms. To the best of my knowledge, first-time Mr. John D. Rockefeller developed and employed a multi-layered structure with Standard Oil, creating a company of companies while subsidiary companies registered and operated in individual states. Since then just about every large corporation and multi-national conglomerate has used such structure – a holding company that owns multiple companies; each subsidiary company focusing on a product/market and operates locally. If something goes wrong in any subsidiary company, other companies and the parent holding company does not suffer.

The income is kept wherever it provides tax efficiency. For example, most large US companies today have billions of dollars on their books in their foreign subsidiaries. According to media reports, US companies have over $1.5T offshore; yes, over 1.5 Trillion Dollars. IRS cannot touch anything because subsidiary is a foreign company. The paying of dividend would mean bringing money to US and hence a taxable event. But company can transfer this wealth to the share holders without taxation by share-buyback.

Establishing headquarters, an office consists of a telephone line and a secretary, is easy to do at a tax-free location (tax haven). Caribbean Island nations get notoriety, tiny little towns of Switzerland around lakes Lucerne, Zug and Thun are good examples to find such "International Headquarters".

On April 29, 2012, New York Times reported that by establishing an office in Reno, NV, Apple avoided California taxes, billions at 9% rate. California Franchise Tax Board cannot do anything. When state has billions in deficit, the only thing state can do is to raise taxes on self proprietary businesses. If that's not enough, cut the programs that provide food or any help to the poor homeless – they don't pay taxes anyway, why should they get help!

Small business owner neither can establish offices in tax havens nor can they do offshore finances. They don't need to; I will explain in chapter 5.

Administrative Tasks

Before I conclude this chapter, let me also review briefly some administrative tasks, i.e., registering the company, getting EIN etc. Some sole proprietary business owners may feel overwhelmed by thinking how to get necessary forms and where to file them. In this section I will try to simplify this work. But keep in mind that because this is administrative work, by definition it is "boring" and somewhat bureaucratic. It must be done; procrastination may result into serious repercussions and loss of some very desirable attributes. The good news is these are one-time tasks and simple enough.

Many advertisements are placed from a number of consultants and attorneys who provide such services. These consultants and attorneys charge few thousand dollars, while the work is trivial. There isn't much to begin with and on top of that these forms are easily amended. Hence, person should not worry about making a mistake. I recommend person to read, learn and do it himself/herself; it will save much important cash, as well as person will know exactly what he/she has done. I also recommend (strongly), that person checks the local and state business laws and ordinance to avoid any surprises.

Registration

Although, I suggested against sole proprietary designation, for the completeness, registration of a **sole-proprietary** company is done at the city-hall or at the county office if person lives in a rural area. Many cities/counties also require registration of the name and a public announcement. It is called declaration of business and its fictitious name; such and such "doing business as" followed by the name of the business. Public announcement is easily accomplished by a small ad in a weekly or bi-weekly ad-magazine/newspaper that we receive in the weekly junk mail. One can ask the registering clerk at the City-Hall/County office how and where to place ad to fulfill this formality, they maintain a list of such magazines/newspapers with all necessary information including charges of such ads (costs about $25).

In most cases, licensing/registration form is also available on city/county web-site. However, I recommend a trip to the office, talking to the clerk and also collecting advisory brochure/publications for new business owners. City/county expects that in future business will provide taxes, revenue to the city/county. In a sense, new business owner is a customer. Hence, city/county provides valuable information and willing to answer any question new business owner may have.

Registration of **C Corporation** is done with the office of the secretary of state in individual states. Once again, while all forms can be obtained from the web-site, I recommend a trip if it's within an hour's commute. People often worry about registering the company in their home state, particularly if it is California or New York. They seek registration in a low-tax state such as Delaware. I will address it in chapter 5.

The reason large companies register in a state like Delaware because these companies do business in multiple states. Few states allow remote office – registration in one state while doing business in multiple states. Even in this situation, depending upon the requirements of other states and the businesses of large corporation, often, they register in multiple states.

At the time of registration, office of the secretary of state also checks whether the name is available. Another business with same name is not registered in one state. It is similar to web domain name; the Internet Service Provider (ISP) checks if the domain name is available before one can register it. Obviously, if there are multiple states, then the name must be checked in all states; more states means more checking.

Registration requires address too. If it is a small business such as a store or a restaurant and person already has a location than using that address is the simplest thing. But if a location has not been selected, at the time of registration, person can use his/her address as a place holder. If it is service business, starting from home is the best choice; person can continue doing so until business become large enough to require a full-time office and employees. If business is based upon a new concept that requires prototype and proof of concept; while prototype is being built by a contractor, house/garage is a good starting place (a standard practice in the Silicon Valley).

In any situation, if part of the house is used, company should pay rent to the home owner. This rent can be deferred but in that case, a promissory debt note should be drawn. As mentioned earlier, person should not mix personal finances with business and a proper paper trail should be maintained.

Bank and Employment Identification Number (EIN)

EIN is issued by the IRS. This is the tax id of the business. As soon as business is registered, person needs to submit IRS form SS-4 to get EIN; IRS website allows it over the Internet. Once EIN is obtained, person should establish a bank account in the name of company using this EIN. For an initial deposit, person can give a "loan" to the company but again as mentioned earlier, a promissory note should be drawn. From this point on, company has its own account and checkbook; personal check or finances should not be mixed. Person is an employee (CEO), company should reimburse if any expenses are paid by a personal check or by the credit card.

Chapter 3: Non Profit Organization

The discussion in Chapter 2 is on for-profit organization. Structuring of operating expenses as discussed in chapter 2 is good, but this time around, good is not enough. When executives of for-profit-corporations throw a million dollar party and media finds out, they get bad-rep; armatures! We don't want any such mishap. Let's look at a better structure, the non-profit organizations. Non-profits are charitable organizations, what they have to do with taxes? Everything!

Red Cross

Red Cross is possibly the most recognized charitable organization in the world. As information is public, it is easy for me to use it as an example. There is one another reason, I am choosing this as an example; I will explain that reason later.

In the tax filing, form 990, part III, the mission is listed as, "The American National Red Cross, a humanitarian organization led by volunteers and guided by its congressional charter and the fundamental principle of the International Red Cross movement, will provide relief to victims of disaster and help people prevent, prepare for, and respond to emergencies."

Let's start with grants and assistance Red Cross provided. In 2010, tax filing, Red Cross listed a total of $81,749,998 for grants and assistance to individuals in the United States (Part IX, the Statement of Functional Expenses, line 2); and $300,552,000 for grants and assistance to governments, organizations and individuals outside the United States (Part IX, line 3).

In the schedule F, the grants and assistance to organizations outside the United States is disclosed. For the year 2010, Red Cross listed 74 grants, given for disaster preparedness, disaster recovery, disaster response and general health. These recipient organizations being recognized charities in the foreign countries and recognized as tax exempt by the IRS. The list is given in table 1. The sum of grants listed in Table 1 is $280,760,855.

Table 1: Grants and other assistance to organizations or entities outside the United States. From Red Cross 2010 tax filing, Schedule F, form 990.

Cent Am/Caribbean	$25,086	Cent Am/Caribbean	$5,295,025
E. Asia/Pacific	$561,655	Cent Am/Caribbean	$1,285,000
Europe/Iceland/Greenland	$125,840	Cent Am/Caribbean	$500,000
Cent Am/Caribbean	$120,008	Cent Am/Caribbean	$191,772
E. Asia/Pacific	$206,000,000	Cent Am/Caribbean	$136,400
Mid East/N. Africa	$14,284	Cent Am/Caribbean	$2,985,834
Russia	$172,677	Cent Am/Caribbean	$1,196,818
Sub-Sahara Africa	$367,738	Cent Am/Caribbean	$1,318,993
Russia	$31,680	Cent Am/Caribbean	$1,049,094
Sub-Sahara Africa	$100,104	Cent Am/Caribbean	$116,721
S. Asia	$9,040	Cent Am/Caribbean	$3,821,078

Region	Amount	Region	Amount
Sub-Sahara Africa	$101,176	S. Asia	$110,427
North America	$507,190	Cent Am/Caribbean	$279,663
S. Asia	$49,921	South America	$187,073
E. Asia/Pacific	$772,000	Russia	$701,069
Cent Am/Caribbean	$35,221	Cent Am/Caribbean	$133,376
Europe/Iceland/Greenland	$7,937,083	Sub-Sahara Africa	$100,307
Europe/Iceland/Greenland	$2,464,256	S. Asia	$986,331
Russia	$49,700	Russia	$21,374
Cent Am/Caribbean	$252,557	Sub-Sahara Africa	$646,637
Russia	$49,442	E. Asia/Pacific	$195,094
Cent Am/Caribbean	$80,000	Russia	$17,477
South America	$91,000	Sub-Sahara Africa	$129,778
South America	$93,506	Russia	$362,789
E. Asia/Pacific	$2,049,903	E. Asia/Pacific	$195,565
South America	$461,053	Cent Am/Caribbean	$3,312,029
Cent Am/Caribbean	$364,151	Cent Am/Caribbean	$2,686,164
South America	$79,470	Cent Am/Caribbean	$6,257,770
Cent Am/Caribbean	$102,895	Cent Am/Caribbean	$928,638
Cent Am/Caribbean	$32,187	Cent Am/Caribbean	$1,826,488
South America	$93,576	Cent Am/Caribbean	$1,376,876
Cent Am/Caribbean	$3,186,416	Cent Am/Caribbean	$144,746
Cent Am/Caribbean	$1,669,632	Cent Am/Caribbean	$1,500,200
Cent Am/Caribbean	$5,763,295	Cent Am/Caribbean	$61,001
Cent Am/Caribbean	$5,238,387	Cent Am/Caribbean	$273,317
E. Asia/Pacific	$899,937	Cent Am/Caribbean	$149,802
S. Asia	$220,348	Cent Am/Caribbean	$107,715

In this list, the recipients of 37 grants are Central America/Caribbean; the total amount is $53,804,355. Although, the word Haiti is not listed but it is fair to assume that the majority of these grants were for the Haiti disaster.

Now, let's also look at the total revenue and expenses, this is Part I of form 990. Line 12 specifies total revenue as $3,452,960,387 (let's call it $3.45B); line 18 specifies total expenses as $3,422,010,386 (let's call it $3.42B). The detailed breakdown of expenses is given in Part IX, the Statement of Functional Expenses. I will get to that in a minute. Let me just complete the Part I of form 990.

The line 13 is grants and similar amounts (combined US and non-US), it is $382,301,998; line 17, other expenses are $1,345,550,396; line 15 is salaries, other compensation, employee benefits, it is $1,694,157,992 (let's call it $1.69B).

Now, readers might be getting the idea, where I am going with all this – yes, 49% of the total revenue ($1.69B out of $3.45B) went directly to employees. Other expenses (in future, I will use the term operating expenses), are almost 39% of the total revenue (almost $1.35B out of $3.45B). The amount of grants for the victims, the primary objective of the charity is only about $382M, 11% of the total revenue – dime on a dollar!

Is it that bad? Please remember that this is the good charity. It is the Red Cross; not a charity of some individual celebrity. Whenever a disaster strikes, you, the middle class, open your heart and give freely. You really need to ask yourself who you are giving to, to the victims or to the employees of the charity.

In Part IX, line 8 is pension plan contribution, the amount itself is $92,008,268 - $92M for the pension of employees, while the sum of 37 grants to Central America/Caribbean (assuming it is Haiti) is $53.8M. Under liabilities, pension and post retirement is listed as $672,134,249; this is where your future donations will go.

In the same section, Part IX, line 9 is other employee benefits, that amount is $164,989,964; and line 11g, fees for other non-employee services is $169,502,436. Forget salary/wages and pension of the employees, the "other" (employee and non-employee), itself is $334,492,400, 120% of all grants listed in table 1.

Not to be confused, I did mention earlier the amount listed on line 2 and line 3 of part IX; that totals to $382,301,998. Interested readers should check, the tax filing as well as audited financial statements is available on the website (I want to be brief).

The breakdown of Functional Expenses includes travel, legal, management, office expenses, equipment purchase etc. that one can understand. The other expenses are for you to decipher.

About half of the grants in Table 1 are of less than $250,000. Schedule J lists a number of employees; every one of them has compensation of more than $300,000. The number of individuals who received over $100,000 is given as 1078.

Didn't mission statement say, "led by volunteers"? You, the middle class Americans, who really volunteer and cleanup after a tornado or hurricane should demand equivalent salaries.

When you look into charity of individual celebrities, make sure you are sitting down and have a glass of cold water handy. You can't get explanation of other expenses from Red Cross; when it is some individual's charity, you won't even get an explanation of any expenses including salaries, retirement and operating expenses. The tax filings are confidential and IRS can't do a thing when there are supporting receipts; IRS cannot dictate how much is being spend where.

Now, you understand why I took your time entertaining operating expenses of for-profit-corporations in chapter 2. The non-profit corporations are no different. If for-profit-corporation gets a bad-rep because of 1-million dollar party; non-profit corporations have 2-million dollars or 3-million dollars party; they call it charity ball and in-fact get praise.

You should reconsider any donation to any charity if the tax filing and audited financial statement are not public. Review financial statement and tax filing. A real charity should not have any salary/retirement/benefits for its executives; operating expenses should be fully spelled-out and contain only essential items. You are donating for the benefit of victims, 90% of your donation should go directly to the victims.

Charity is a good business. Because the amount in salary of an employee becomes personal income to that employee, it is taxed as personal income but there is no restriction on how much is the salary. Business income (business revenue) is even better; it is completely tax exempt; business can grow tax-free! Employees, particularly executives at a charity are not doing any charity, they are pursuing their careers like anybody else; they draw huge salary/retirement/benefits without any restriction.

The only thing is that executives of non-profit corporation have not been able to make hundreds of millions or billions of dollars. I didn't say they can't; I said, they haven't been able to do so. They haven't figured it out yet; I guess these talented executives are not so talented after-all. Don't worry, I won't write and educate them.

It is time for you to donate to yourself; charity starts from home.

Start a new career; start a new charity. You want to travel around the world, as an executive of the charity, go right-ahead. If you find a location you really like and want to go there often, buy a property and make it the foreign office of the charity. Wining-dining is just peanuts, no problem there; think big ticket items, they are yours under the operating expenses.

Forget for Profit Corporation, that's so past century. In the 21st century, we don't care for profit, we run non-profit corporation. Yes, it is time for you to set-up a tax exempt non-profit business, I will explain in chapter 5.

In The Name of God

From the title of this section, some may think of the traditional advice – donation to church is tax deductible. No, I am not giving any such advice; instead, I am saying stop donating to church.

Church used to ask for 10%; that was to pray to God that you and your kids may not go hungry when 1/3rd of your income goes to the federal government; 10% to state like CA and NY; 5% local (in various forms like property taxes); and rest in sales taxes, gasoline taxes, tobacco taxes, alcohol tax (marijuana is free; in CA, you can grow it in your home).

Only God can save you. Hindu Vashnevs have 8.6 million gods and goddesses, but there is no god of taxes! The whole thing stinks to high heavens; where is god, when you need him?

Some sentences and expressions in this section may anger few readers; but before you start sending hate mail, consider the fact that I have nothing against any religion. My objective is to illustrate how to eliminate taxes; I am merely drawing examples to get my point across.

May God have mercy on my soul! Whatever I am writing has nothing to do with God, its man.

In the wild west, there was a saying – if you want money, rob a bank. Well, we are not robbing anyone, they are. We will deal with banks; besides banks, where else is the money – riches are in churches and temples. Banks are novice rich, churches and temples are ole-money. Neither individual nor corporations can come close to the riches of churches/temples – gold and silver objects, jewels, art, wood and stone carvings, real-estate, cash and other investments worldwide and everything is well protected. I am not referring Vatican in Rome that is a country in itself, beyond the Yankees laws. I am talking in general, the churches and temples all over the world of various religions. In old days, it was the wealth of temples that lured attacks of other civilizations.

In 1985, a scandal broke-out in Oregon. Five years earlier, an religious "guru", Rajneesh, set-up an Ashram and racked-up hundreds of millions; over 90 Roll Royce cars, large amount of real estate, any and every luxury you can imagine. Everything tax exempt, contributions from the faithful. Scandal broke-out because one evening, a secretary took $43M (loose change) and went away. In 2008, another such "guru, Mahesh Yogi, died leaving an estate worth £2B. Interested readers can look-up details on the Internet.

Setting up an Ashram and collecting 100-Rolls is an exceptional talent, at par with Wall-Street executive (probably better); indeed, it deserves millions. Growing up, I remembered plenty of cases when someone had an apparition (sometimes in sleep), demanding certain things and apparition rested only after neighbors gave enough donations. There was one another solution that I liked quite a bit – call the local exorcist and with a broom, beat the sh** out, literally. You can't do that in America; exorcists here just jump around, won't even qualify for dance on Got Talent show.

My point is, the amount of money is enormous in the name of God; any name, any religion, anywhere on Earth; it always has been and it always will be. People care more about after-life than the present-life.

One of the prime reasons of any religion is to obtain individual peace. Story is told that after being baptized by John, Jesus lived in a cave and meditated. Often, he also left his disciples, went alone in a desolate place to meditate. Siddhartha meditate under a tree in a jungle away from everything. In all Hindu stories, every Rishi (intelligent teacher living like a monk) lived in Ashrams in jungle. Very simple life and meditation, rest of the time dedicated in teaching and welfare of the public; no money involved. Today, they don't; people in India are corrupt, it is virtually impossible to get anything done at a government office unless first you pay the tribute (bribe is bad English) to the whole hierarchy of gods in that office.

In stories of ancient India, King and commoner alike, used to give-up everything and go to the Himalayas to meditate, to live in peace and harmony. The reasoning was same as written masterfully by Ralph Waldo Emerson.

But all churches and temples are glittering and luxurious places. Whether it is a church altar or a deity in a temple, they are all laden with gold, silver and jewels, intricate wood and stone carvings and art work. Do you really think you can meditate in such a place? Meditation is out of the question, just looking around, mind is blown away. Unless of-course, meditation technology has changed and new technology requires blown mind. Modern meditation seems to require a place glided with gold, silver, diamonds, rubies and sapphires. Physically, no man has seen the soul or the heaven, so we don't know about soul going to heaven. For the physical world, churches and temples are indeed tax heavens (havens) anyone can enjoy!

Whenever I see a picture of any Bishop or Cardinal, I see a person clad in silk and laden with gold and silver, often with diamonds, rubies and sapphires. Isn't directly opposite to what Jesus taught? Story is told that in the courtyard of the temple in Jerusalem, Jesus denounced such riches and even toppled the tables of Pharisees.

Not just in Christianity, in other religions as well, the key figure has denounced the wealth. Siddhartha, founder of Buddhism, abandoned his kingdom. People familiar with Indian history would also know that the emperor Samudragupta Morya denounced kingdom and became Buddhist monk.[1]

Only Jews don't have any story of denouncing wealth; there is an understandable reason. Yahweh had direct business dealing with Jews. He knew they need help; parent helping the weakest kid. They were common people – shepherd, carpenters etc.; whoever

---

[1] *Chandragupta Morya repelled the attack of Alexandra and established a dynasty that consolidated and ruled over the entire India; Samudragupta was the grand son of Chandragupta.*

and whenever feels like it, bullied them. Assyrian, Minoan, Hittite, Babylonian, Persian, Egyptian, Greek, Roman, all the way to modern times, they never seem to get a break and live in peace.[2] Only Solomon could have denounced money and kingdom but when beautiful woman is around, queen of Sheba, you want to show-off; that's no time to become a monk. God tried to help them, gave land to Abraham, tax-free, but what else can He do.

I am not talking here denouncing anything; enough of our money is taken away as it is. I am talking here to learn from religion, doesn't matter which religion. Religions are there to teach us, don't they?

I am not talking what the priests, preachers, bishops and cardinals say, but what is written in the books. I am not a religious scholar, there is a possibility of digression, so, let me simplify. Doesn't matter which religion, each has a number of popular stories of fight between the Good and the Evil. In these stories,

---

[2] *They just don't get a break, even I can poke them!*

Good finally win by the intelligence and wisdom. Even the stories of King Solomon and King Arthur are stories of intelligence and wisdom. Entertaining as they may be, the moral of all these stories is to use your intelligence to fight evil. We are not talking here physical annihilation that is Hollywood.

Every religion teaches reasoning. Jesus questioning Pharisees is reasoning, what he taught to the apostles is same reasoning. Conversion of Saul is meditation, back and forth argument and reasoning; later, Saint Paul's teaching is same reasoning.

It surprises me when in Buddhist temples, I see people enchanting a line or two of half Hindi and half Sanskrit; enchanting for hours without even knowing what it means. The word Buddha means the person who has Buddhi, intelligence. The word Gottem is made of two words – Guru (teacher) and uttem (excellent); meaning excellent teacher. Every one of us cannot be Gottem but every one of us has Buddhi, intelligence; the question is how one uses it. The primary teaching of Siddhartha, Gottem is to ask questions, reason it out and do what is reasonable.

Do not follow anything blindly, including whatever I have written!

Hindu Puranas are full of stories of fights between demons and gods. In just about all those stories demons are more powerful and have better weapons, but gods win by intelligence. There are also some stories about competition among gods; in those stories as well, the winner is who used intelligence rather than force.

Greek gods were lot more complicated but many popular stories are again stories of intelligence. When no option is found year after year, the use of hollow wooden horse in the Trojan War was an outstandingly clever move.

My point is, as common people, you neither have authority nor do power; rich and law makers have both. Use of intelligence is the only option. Learn the rules of the game, use the rules that cannot be switched on you and use them to your advantage.

Every religion teaches this – become religious. I am not talking another church of the Christ or temple of God. Think in terms of the temple of Sheldon Cooper or possibly the church of Raj. The Hindi word Raj means kingdom. Hence, the church of Raj means church of (my) kingdom; that has good prospective. Worship Hindu goddess Laxmi; Laxmi is money. We are talking money, so worship money, why bother with any other god?

In God We Trust: anything and everything done in the name of God is tax exempt!

Become Saint, Saints have divine powers; IRS can't tax Saints, nobody can. I will explain in chapter 5.

Chapter 4: Children Are the Future

Mentioning children invokes emotions; hence, anything and everything is done in the name of children's education. Besides billions of dollars from the state and the federal government (that is your money), you also pay tuition – really, that is double taxation on you. But the real question is how much of it is really used in the direct benefit to your children? Think about it without being emotional for a minute. Everyone uses the word "investment in the children's future"; if it is an investment, investment decisions are better when investor is not emotional.

Schools and universities are also non-profit organizations. A charity may or may not get government funding, schools and universities get billions. If charity organizations take 50% for their employees and another 40% in the operating expenses, schools and universities take it all, 100%. Yes, teachers and professors are perusing their career; they are not doing any charity. I understand, they are middle class Americans doing jobs and they do teach children. So, saying 100% is not really fair; nonetheless, it is salary to the employees. Rest of the money is of-course present and future operating expenses.

Children do get education from teachers and professors, so let's take their salary out of the discussion for the time being. Does hundreds of thousands of dollars, often million dollar salaries of university Presidents and Chancellors helps in the learning of children? University Presidents, Provost, Chancellors, VPs, Deans don't teach anything; kids don't even see them ever, except may be at the convocation. Besides very large salaries, they all have hefty budgets of millions of dollars. Yes, you guessed it right – not just for wining and dining but also for country club memberships, travel around the world, the other "operating expenses".

Does a billion dollar building contribute to the learning of children? I am not saying that kids should sit in a tent, but billion dollars on building! In my elementary education, in the 3rd and the 5th grades, I in-fact had a tent classroom. It wasn't some remote Indian village; it was a large metro and historically important very well known town. Enrollment unexpectedly shot-up, school just didn't have space; limiting enrollment and letting go kids was unheard of, that was the correct emotion. As a kid, where I am sitting was not even on my conscious. Even at undergraduate engineering college, many classrooms have broken windows. Dorm rooms were damp because of the flood in the nearby river few months ago. That was just fine; we were there to learn engineering. College was new and was lacking laboratory facilities. Hence, for experimental work/education/experience, we were sent to one of the best engineering college in India, one of the Indian Institute of Technology. Guess what, they also had broken windows.

I am not saying that kids in America should be subjected to such conditions. My point is fancy building doesn't do anything in learning. Marble floors in the hallway, wood paneled rooms don't teach, probably they are distractions in learning. Money spend on ritzy building is a waste. If it had any contribution in the kid's learning, dropout rate in the ritzy schools would be zero and graduating students would be advance and more knowledgeable than anyone else. American schools would not be in the last-few in education among industrialized nations or behind many developing countries. In every election, there is one or more measure to issue a bond for education, to erect yet another fancy building. Politicians and school administrators of-course advocate for these bond measures in the name of education of the children. These bonds are additional taxes on you. Stop approving these bond measures; you are increasing your own taxes and wasting your dollars.

If you want to spend this amount for the education of your kid, hire a tutor – money will be spend for the learning of your kid. A number of companies provide online tutoring. Because of the large pool of highly educated people and low salaries in comparison to the United States, these companies assign foreign teachers/tutors to US students. Students pay a small fee and get one-on-one help on any subject they need, help using real-time Internet communication. Enroll your kid in their program. Do you care if a teacher is sitting half way across the globe, or the future of your kids? Except of-course American teachers will cry out that I am proposing to create jobs in other countries because I am saying how bad and yet expensive they really are. As parent, your responsibility is good education of your children, not the welfare of teachers or school administrators. Get education that is at the global par, after graduation your kids will be able to compete at the global level in businesses, in jobs or whatever endeavor they peruse; isn't that what you want?

I wish we could outsource legislative jobs too; we could get rid of expensive and useless congress.

I even want to suggest that the parents who can effort personal monitoring should dump the traditional schools and enroll their kids to online schools. Monitoring is needed because of the kid's attention span and motivation. Over 30 states have online schools; these are American companies. Today, self-motivated students, parents conducting at-home education and adult students use these courses effectively.

In general, online courses are of very high quality and taught in simple language that students comprehend, in a manner that keeps students engaged. Online courses developed by Salman Khan are good examples of high quality delivered in easily understandable form (more than 2400 courses on Math, Physics, Chemistry, Biology, History, Business and Finance are available for free at www.khanacademy.org). Ask your kid's Math or Physics teacher to do problems given in Khan's courses; you might be up for a surprise. Other examples are K12.com and PA cyber. Some companies also have employees/teachers conducting such online courses; this brings monitoring. Company and teachers focus on teaching and monitor the progress of every single student; the word "class size" is irrelevant. Education using online courses is uniform education and at a fraction of the cost what you pay to traditional schools.

Similar to crummy building, throughout my education, I don't recall any teacher who had class size on his/her conscious. Each section of each grade in various schools I attended, had 60-70 kids in the class, some even 100. Focus of all teachers and kids was on what is being taught and what is learned.

At Case Western Reserve University, I myself taught undergraduate Computer Engineering classes (Assembly Language, Data Structure, Logic Design) with over 100, even over 150 students in some semesters. At San Jose State University class size was limited to 30; when I proposed to let more students register in my class, department chairman over-ruled. My time was not the issue, politics was.

It would have sent disastrous, in-fact dangerous ripples throughout the system. Case Western Reserve is a private university, large class size was permitted; San Jose State is public university, small class size is a bargaining chip to get more money from the State. More money from the state is basically more money from you – your tax dollars.

In various schools, a number of administrators even advocate class size of 20 or less. Let's say, if class size is 30, do you think education level will go down compare to when class size is 35? If it does, that teacher should not be teaching in the first place.

By making loud noise for small class size, more money can be obtained. It's very simple; whoever shouts louder, gets attention. By shouting louder more taxes, more money can be siphoned-off, all in the name of children.

I have also seen teachers leading kids to protesting rallies, rallies for the increased salary and more benefits – their cause. Surprisingly, TV stations reported it in the local news, but no one questioned. Rally of little elementary school kids invokes emotions. Elementary school kids, about 10-years old, don't have any understanding that they are being used. Parents should be outraged – this is child abuse, to get more money.

Earlier I hold-on discussion on teacher's salary; lets look at it. The website of National Education Association contains detailed data on university faculty salaries (www.nea.org/he); interested readers should look at the magazine Advocate and Almanac. 2012 Almanac, table 1, provides comparison of average salaries 40-years ago; year 1972-73 and 2010-11. The percentage change in constant dollars is: Professors 447.3%; Associate Professor 414.9%; Assistant Professor 424.5%, Instructor 441.9%; even lecturers and no rank have percentage increase of almost 350%. In graph, this increase shows as a straight-up line; no dips, not even a flattening point anywhere. Teacher's salary is investment in kid's education; I don't know any investment (stocks, bonds, commodities, real estate) that has appreciated over 400% in such a steady manner. What the heck Wall Street is doing? They should be selling faculty salary backed derivatives!

At the same time, educational standard went down and still going down steadily. Increased teacher's salary doesn't improve education.

The lecturers and no-rank are generally referred to part-time faculty, who often work full-time at a company but teach a course. In my experience at San Jose State University, these were experienced (10-15 years), working engineers in hi-tech Silicon Valley companies with Ph. D. and MS degrees. They were paid less than $10,000 per course.

Now, think for a moment – if a practitioner engineer with an equivalent degree can teach for less than $10,000, why would you want to pay someone $100,000 to $150,000 to teach the same 4-to-6 courses (in "teaching" universities, a professor teaches 6-courses in a year; in "research" university, a professor teaches 4-courses per year and expected to write couple of papers each year)? I am also aware of some universities hire part-time instructors and pay only about $5000 per course. Even at $10,000 per course; it is $60,000 a year for 6-courses!

By the way, whenever a professor gets a research grant, his/her teaching load is reduced – it is called "course buying"; university takes part of the grant money (in addition to the overhead), in lieu of reduced courses. With large research grant, a professor can even buy all courses, teaching nothing at-all.

There is one more way to look at it, this I have said in multiple presentations at various conferences: teaching 3-courses per semester means 9-hours/week of lecture time. Let's add 1-hour per course per week for preparation.

Anything more should be unacceptable when teaching the same course again and again.[3] Professor also needs to assign office hours; it is generally 1-to-2 hours per week, let's put 3-hours. For grading homework and labs, they have teaching assistants.[4] Hence, total work time is 15-hours per week. Let's add 30% extra time for "coffee and relaxation"; it is still 20-hours per week. Not to mention 3-months of summer is completely free (we don't call vacation, that's bad English).

My point is if you think by paying more taxes, new bonds for schools buildings, higher salary to teachers, your kid will get decent education in public

---

[3] *I memorized Electrical Engineering books cover-to-cover after teaching a course couple of times. Not just me, with a weekly 10-minutes guidance session per team of 2-3 students each, students designed complete computer chips as part of their class projects (projects didn't remain on paper); students were there to learn.*

[4] *I wanted to grade home works myself, so I told I don't need any grader. But department Chairman assigned one anyway. He has to spend it because it was in the budget. Un-spend money in the budget is surplus and impermissible in any government organization.*

schools, than you are delusional. The salary data I mentioned above is very compelling.

At college level you can't; but at K12 level, consider taking your kid out of the system. If you take your kid out of the system and get international teachers, your kid will get decent education, guaranteed, it will be at global par.

Smaller number of students in a public school means less money from the state; less wastage of your tax dollars. In principle, if everyone in a community takes his/her kid out of the local school, school will be shut down. Will it reduce your taxes? I doubt it. My conjecture is that taxes will remain the same. Eliminate your taxes altogether, it is the only choice available.

Let's also look at universities and what happens to billions of dollars universities receive from state. If university doesn't receive the desired amount, chancellor can order to limit new admissions. University can fill a large portion of this reduced number by international students who can pay higher tuition further disfranchising in-state students. When it comes to their job, it is American jobs; but when it is more money, they cater to foreign students!

When eligible in-state students don't get admission, all they can do is protest and thus pressure to increase university funding. Nobody questions that the reason of the existence of state universities is to educate in-state students.

Another item of contention is retirement (pension). In Cal State and UC system, a professor with $100,000 salary gets about $15,000 towards retirement; contribution in the pension plan. In comparison, for-profit-companies provide 3%-to-7% matching contribution in the retirement plan (401K); even the best of companies limit to 7%. Of-course, if someone even mentions the word "pension reform", teachers start shouting. You may be getting $3000-4000 contribution in your 401K but you are providing double or triple of that amount in retirement of your kid's teacher; while kid is getting irrelevant education.

Besides large salaries, presidents and other administrators of universities have been reported to lavishness similar to the corporate executives I mentioned in chapter 2; universities also have operating expenses, don't they. These are not recent practices. In 1992 book, "Imposters in the Temple", Martin Anderson gave a number of university examples of such lavishness. Most likely, he was expecting that after reading those examples, people will take some action. People did take action. Today, such practices are so wide spread that country club memberships, wining and dining is not even considered lavishness; it is the norm by Deans, VPs, Provost and Presidents of universities. If middle class kids are drowned in student loans while getting irrelevant education that won't get them a job, it is their stupidity. Education is a noble profession; universities need more money for the nobilities. Once again, law makers in Washington and in state capitol are sleeping; as long as money doesn't go into personal account, IRS can't do a thing.

To the Protesting Students: You are grown-ups, think for a minute and ask yourself – if money is given, where will it go and how much? Will it really go to your education? Or $2/3^{rd} - 3/4^{th}$ will go to the university employees in increased salary, benefits and retirement?

They will get increased salary/benefits/retirement; if it isn't from the state (your parents tax dollars), they will raise your tuition and get it from you.

When a university reduces and limits enrollment, and at the same time hikes tuition, none of the government official or state assembly member even flinch. Instantaneous 30% increase in the price of goods and services at a business would be called price grouching for any business. Where is the law – I guess sleeping, as usual!

Students are drowned in student loans, already over Trillion dollars and they haven't in the "real world" yet. They will be paying out this loan for the rest of their lives; nice head-start don't you think! That's not the worst part – the worst part is that the loan is unforgivable. No matter what, including personal bankruptcy, student loan will not be wiped clean. Personal bankruptcy wipes clean all personal debt but not the student loan. Your blood will be sucked till death; yes, if student loan is not paid, it will be deducted when you retire and get social security.

Death and Taxes: I have been writing that taxes can be avoided; it is the student loan that you cannot avoid. Benjamin Franklin didn't even know the term "student loan"; Death is of-course the will of God; I did talk about God, didn't I?

Oh yes, law makers won't let interest rate to double, to over 6%, on student loan. Over 6% in the free market economy, when the Federal Reserve rate is 0% or even 30-year bond interest rates hovering around 4%, it itself shows how rigged the system is.

But the government won't let your interest rate double; government will "subsidize" student loans. Hey, if you really want to subsidize, give it at the Federal Reserve rate; you give money to banks at that rate, don't you?

At the time of this writing, the senate has already rejected proposal on student loan interest rates. They will keep going back-and-forth to keep it as a distraction. Make no mistake, student loan interest rates is a pure distraction, designed to take your eyes off the main item. Yes, interest rate has an effect; you won't feel that effect until you start paying back. Even if they keep the interest rate as it is; the main item is the Principal, the amount you are forced to borrow to pay excessive tuition. If there is no excessive tuition, will you be borrowing? Some may have to, but it will not be as large an amount as you are forced to borrow now.

In previous chapters, my advice to eliminate taxes is basically for people who are working, your parents for example. You are not paying taxes yet, your parents are. You are still in school; most of what I wrote in previous chapters and early part of this chapter doesn't affect you yet, in a broader sense. What affects you is much bigger sh** than the working middle class Americans – your whole working life has been mortgaged, sliced and diced, even before you start working.

Some of you may say we already know this; what you don't know is that they are also going to sell you just like they did for homes of your parents. Yes, I am talking **student loan backed derivatives**, second derivatives and credit swap. Bundle student loans, slice them, dice them, fu** them and sell them all over the world. Just like they did home mortgage loans backed derivatives. The loan guarantee for mortgage backed derivatives was houses; lot of people walked out leaving their houses. They lost their homes but at-least they could start over. With student loan, you can't walk out; loan guarantee is you and by law you can't default. You can walkout only when you go to heaven (die). Countries can default on their debt, even the United States; you can't. This is pure gold, 26K, beyond anything they ever had or even imagined; given to them by law. Coming soon, when student loans backed derivatives will hit the market, rating companies like Moody and S&P will happily give AAAA++++ ratings.

You are still in school, your whole life has been trashed, guaranteed by law that you can't get out, you don't have a choice.

Law is sleeping as usual. No wait, law is not sleeping; it is busy creating distractions (like interest rate on student loan), so that you won't focus on the main item – the good cop, bad cop routine.

You are grown-up, play their game; playing better than them is the only choice you have. And you know what, you can; in-fact, you can play much better, much much better than the tax elimination as I have written in the previous chapters.

Don't turn to violence, violence doesn't achieve anything.

Fundamental problem is again large amount of money. If you play it right, instead of giving, you can take their money!

Play the game, use your brain and beat them in their own game – take their shirt and sell it. Someone got to do it; your parents (working people) can't, you can. Children are the future, new generation always has new options; options, these old boys can't do a thing about. I will explain in chapter 5.

Should I have not written it in a book? They will read it too. Have a sporting spirit, you are playing game – play with an in-your-face attitude, they can't do a thing, unless they shoot in their own foot first.

Chapter 5: Game Plan

You can't fight them, join them; stop giving your money and takeout as much as you can before they completely drain-out the system. Do your job, work hard is conventional wisdom; ditch conventional wisdom. It doesn't work; all moves and their counter moves are known; besides the game is rigged. You need to use either unconventional moves or the moves of your opponents.

Let's discuss some actions to eliminate taxes. In the introduction, my proposition was that middle class America should pay zero taxes. Let's start with state taxes, it is simple.

State Taxes

If your state takes away your money in state taxes, there is no need to live there. Certainly, there is no need to live in the states like California and New York who take away almost 10%; not a single person should be living there. Move out. Move to a state that has no state taxes like Nevada, Texas, Wyoming, Florida, Alaska etc. Most billionaires call such states their home. Every time, Forbes list come out, local news papers and TV stations proudly announce how many billionaire "call" such and such city their home. The only exception may be Warren Buffet. He lives in Omaha, what does he know, he even wants to tax the rich. There is only one word to describe him – reasonable. You want to play a rigged game, don't be reasonable; law makers don't listen to reasonable people.

Moving out doesn't mean selling your home, putting your furniture and other personal belongings in a truck and go. Take a short vacation. Go to Vegas, have a drink and play some poker (you'll learn not to flinch with my game plan); go to Miami and swim in the ocean (water in San Francisco is too cold); go to Orlando and visit Disney parks (objective is serious, no goofing around); go to Huston and enjoy warm waters of the gulf (Huston will not have any problem); go to Yellow Stone, a bear might walk in front of you (watch bare necessities of your life); go to Alaska and see glaciers (you might also see Russia); go to any such place that fancy you. The only constraint is that it should be in a state that has no taxes.

While enjoying your vacation, rent a place, possibly a studio apartment. There are plenty of low rent studio apartments available everywhere, it doesn't matter if there are 10 members in your family – you are not going to live there; you are going to "call" it your home. Another possibility is to rent a room with a local resident; with room in a house, you don't need to worry about break-in in the empty studio apartment.

Declare the address of this rental unit your residence. You will require to change your driver's license and car registration, but that is about it. Now, you don't need to pay taxes of your previous state.

For example, if you are a resident of California, drive to Las Vegas or Reno, whichever is easier; rent a room/apartment (plenty are available for around $200/month; some even give free rent for the first month); change your driver's license and the registration of your car; put this address on all your business dealings (income should be at this address); you are set – your California taxes are gone.

This is the basic principle, for small businesses. People having jobs require little bit more work; I will explain later in this chapter.

In God We Trust

In chapter 2, I suggested that all businesses owners including small shops, ranches and farms should establish themselves as C-Corporations and reduce their taxes similar to large corporation. Reduction isn't good enough, let's just eliminate them altogether.

With little imagination and some planning, you can use a better structure, better than C Corporation. There are also certain formalities that one should be aware-of. In a nut-shell, think about a non-profit corporation. I didn't take your time discussing Red Cross, churches/temples and schools/universities for no reason.

Let's start with farmers and ranchers, they can easily implement it on their land – erect a shed anywhere on your farm/ranch and put a cross on its door and the roof. A 10x10 shed is adequate. This is your church. Once you establish your church, assign all your land, home and everything to this church. Don't own anything personally; give everything to God or whatever deity you want to worship. When you give-up your personal belongings and give them to God, God will be pleased and eliminate your taxes. At the end of last chapter, I mentioned to worship Laxmi – the deity of the church is "money", keep the deity in your temple/church, don't give it to the government.

There may be an issue of intellectual property (IP) rights of existing churches/temples. This is why, in chapter 3, I suggested to think in terms of the temple of Sheldon Cooper or the church of Raj. If you use pictures of Jesus and Mary, put a cross over the roof and start accumulating assets; a bishop might come knocking. Put a pawn in the front (a fictitious name), it will block the bishop.

It's a new church, it is understandable that you may not have large congregation; permanent members may be your spouse and children. For small congregation, a 10x10 hall is adequate for common prayer. On special church occasions like child's birthday, invite outside members (your friends and relatives) for the church function. For these other church functions when outside guests are invited, you of-course need larger place, a house.

As soon as property belongs to your church/temple, it is tax exempt and protected. You are now care-taker of the church and its property. Keep doing your work as you have been doing but the income from your farm and ranch now belongs to the church, it is fully tax exempt. Church will use its income to support care taker. You will not be starved and you also have roof over your head – your home is care-taker's living quarters. After supporting care-taker, whatever is left, remains in the church. Your wife/daughter wants jewelry, buy real gold and silver – all churches/temples buy gold/silver jewelry and decorate their deities. Of-course, from time-to-time, a piece of jewelry needs to be removed from the deity for cleaning/repair etc.; care-taker's wife/daughter is wearing it for safe keeping. You want to invest some income in stocks/bonds/real-estate/commodities, go right ahead – it's all church's property. Buy anything; spend/invest any which way you like. You don't need to go off-shore tax havens; haven is on your farm/ranch – finally, Heaven on Earth!

You are employee of the church. Church may give you a small salary, salary at the poverty line. Church funds your retirement in Roth 401K so that the amount is never been taxed. You are the sole care-taker and work 24-hours; hence, you need to live on-site in the house that church owns. Church buys food and clothes for charity purpose; you are the needy poor person, church gives food and clothes to you.

If you still want to keep some money in your name, church can give its care-taker a small salary. I suggest near about $15,000; don't go over the poverty line. This amount you can deposit in your savings.

People living in mobile homes and sheds in the boonies can simply declare their home as church/temple. These homes are essentially one room just like most of the existing neighborhood churches. All questions and complications go away; America becomes the most religious nation on earth.

Besides being tax exempt and worries of the IRS, even large corporations/banks will need to think twice before foreclosing and auctioning-off the church property if mortgage is not paid on-time. Foreclosing and auctioning God's property, will banks have courage to fight against the God?

It is fair to assume that middle class Americans living in cities and suburbs don't have 10,000 sq ft mansions and acres of front/back yards. With few sq yards of front, yet, you still do it literally, then, please keep 30 pieces of silver handy for lobbying to crucify any voice of reason. My recommendation is forget shed, put a cross on the roof of your house and declare the whole house a church – you are now, on-site care-taker of the church; living room is for general gathering of the congregation (family), kitchen is of-course for the food of congregation, one room is to hear confessions (of children), one room is living quarters of the care taker. If you have bigger house with more rooms, get a proper designation of each room.

Charity Starts from Home

This idea of church is a bit cumbersome for people living in regular houses in cities and suburbs. For people living in regular houses, a charity, a cause, is a better proposition. Become unemployed, many people already are. Instead of looking for a job, start you own business. No, I am not suggesting for profit C Corporation, start a non-profit. Work full time but as a volunteer; forget job, that's history.

We are the kindest people human race has ever seen. We want to help not only every poor and mal-nourished kid around the world, but also animals and even insects in the far-away lands! As an employee of non-profit corporation, you can draw your salary (don't draw a large salary), non-profit corporation will of-course pay all "operating expenses". Whatever is earned, whether it is donation or business income, it is within the non-profit umbrella. Money may not be in your name, but still remains in your control. For any reason if you decide to transfer it in your name, you can certainly do that. In the context of C Corporation, I suggested that small business owners leave surplus income in the company. This is what non-profit corporations do by default. There are certain formalities (on paper), but it's your charity, your company and your money.

Philanthropy is such a good career that depending upon what business you are in, you may even get the state and the federal funding. Most rich people have a charitable trust, foundation etc. Whenever they get a chance, they conduct fund raising event for the favorite charity and collect your dollars. Federal and state funding depends upon lobbying; creating a yearly report makes it real official.

In the nation's history, there are very few incidents when the governor of a state was recalled; California is one of them. State had and has billions in deficit but continue to fund hundreds of annual report that have nothing to do with anything. California requiring annual report on the kangaroo population in Australia is just one example – so that money can hop-around. You have heard such examples from every state and federal offices. Terminator didn't terminate production of these reports; I don't know if he knew or not, but wasn't it his responsibility to check what is in the budget? In 2012, Jerry Brown found more than 50 such projects, buried in long obscure documents that nobody reads; most likely many still are. How well you can bury government funding of your charity depends upon your lobbying.

Once you set-up a Charity, advertise it. Go online, show couple of pictures of starving children or dying cats/dogs, it is likely that you will get enough donations to support all kinds of "operating expenses".

Consider charity for the poor aborigine tribal children on Juan Fernandez Islands in the South

Pacific. Don't question me if there is such a tribe. Didn't you read Robinson Crusoe; these children are his descendent. When documents are notarized, stamped and sealed by the government officials, the tribe exists.

But if you don't like my tribe, pick your own; visit them, give them $1.00 per person and take their signatures/thumb-prints. Also take some pictures and certificate from their leader as a precaution. IRS will ask; someone else may also poke few questions. African nations are very popular to find poor people, tribes, animals and insects that need help. Being born in India; India, Bangladesh, Bhutan and Nepal are my favorite nations. Cost used to be $1-$2, with inflation, now it will cost about $10, but you can get official certificate with government seal and everything about your good charity. These are not counterfeit; these are real, signed by the real government officials and stamped with real government seal. Be careful, use local currency and you should never flash money (remain poor); if you flash money, price will go up rapidly.

At-home, because of your kind nature, now, you will be rewarded with additional tax exemptions and immense personal and organizational protection. I am not proposing anything new – celebrities, rich-and-famous do it routinely. You can too, you should too. All you need to do is to get clear in your own mind that employees of non-profit don't do any charity; they receive good salaries, medical, retirement, vacation and all other benefits just like for-profit corporate employees. I did give data in chapter 3 while discussing Red Cross, organization on which data is publicly available – individual's salaries in hundreds of thousands of dollars, who's charity is it? Oh yes, of-course, charity or not, "executive talent" needs millions.

If you really want to do charity, do it yourself. Stop giving donations to a third party. Just like government takes $1/3^{rd}$ of your income in taxes, when you give donation to a third party charity, takes at-least 50% of your money in direct salaries and another 40% in operating expenses; don't be surprised if the amount going to the victims is just 1% or less.

It is time for you to establish your own charity and become its CEO/President. CEO/President of a charity is just an employee of that charity. When you take a salary, your non-profit corporation has to pay payroll taxes and you have to pay personal income taxes; don't take a large salary.

Now, the finesse. When you have your own charity and working there as CEO/President, draw a token salary, close to poverty line. Drawing large salary is just crude and stupid. Whatever you need to operate your life; use operating expenses. Principle is same what I described in chapter 2 while discussing C Corporation; the only change is instead of C Corporation, now you have a non-profit organization.

If you want an additional layer of protection and to become bullet-proof against IRS or anyone else, then also setup a charity trust in the foreign country. Now, your US charity will give grant to the foreign charity that is also recognized as a tax exempt entity by the IRS. Nobody can demand explanation of expenses from foreign charity; if they do, tell them to go to hell, we are doing charity here. Any number of grants and any amount the foreign charity trust receives, how to spend, is its business; it can give all of it to a person, no one can question. IRS can only question US charity, as long as it is giving to another tax exempt entity, nothing they can do.

There are laws and regulations to tax the income of C Corporation; these laws create headache of finding tax havens, shifting money etc. All income of non-profit organization is tax exempt by law, free and clear.

Congress can't change these laws, I dare them. They can't even touch these laws. Non-profit organizations cover just about every rich; they also cover all schools and universities; churches, temples, synagogues and mosques; not to mention that some law-makers and government officials have their own charity. My conjecture is that every influential person in the nation is associated with a non-profit organization in one form or another. Laws and regulation governing non-profit organizations are off-limit, no one can touch them. Don't you see, Saints do charity; Saints have divine powers, no one can mess with the divine power. If anyone even thinks to touch these laws and regulations, person will be thrown out of the system and suffer the divine wrath. In all likelihood, person will be thrown to the dogs, all job/career gone in a second.

Hence, I am suggesting that all middle class Americans join the system. You have heard the expression – CEOs rub elbow with like CEOs (I substituted rich by CEO). Join the club, become a Saint. Right now, you are an outsider. You don't have your own non-profit organization, you deserve to pay taxes.

Jobs Are Gone

A number of constraints come into play for employees. For example, even if they establish their residence in a tax-free state, employer will withhold state taxes – if the company is in California, salary of employee is California income and subjected to California taxes; establishing residency in Nevada doesn't do anything.

Small business owner, farmers and rancher can establish their businesses as non-profit organization whether it is in religious form or a charity. But people doing jobs can't; they work for a company, they don't own it. Employer will also withhold federal and FICA taxes, what can one do?

It is difficult to think how employees can eliminate their taxes; difficult, not impossible.

Don't become employee, when you are not an employee, company will not withheld any taxes. I am not suggesting to quit and become unemployed (that's an option too!), I am suggesting to become a consultant.

Companies will be very resistive to the idea of having full time consultant instead of full time employees. You need to offer them something; indeed, offer them money, a financial incentive to convert you into a consultant. No, don't suggest reduced salary or any such thing. In-fact, you should factor-in the cost of health/life insurance and retirement benefits in the compensation (in the consulting fee); the amount should be same what company spends when you are an employee. The financial incentive to the company is that the company needs not to pay FICA taxes on your behalf when you are a consultant.

Both, worker and the company win when worker is a consultant rather than an employee. I in-fact recommend that all large companies should direct their human resource (HR) department to establish an option for anyone who wants to be a full time consultant instead of employee. Large companies can save a bundle by eliminating their FICA burden; share holders and Wall Street will love it.

Once company agree for you to work as a consultant, move and establish your consultancy company in a tax-free state. Please don't use self proprietary structure; establish a C Corporation. The employer company now giving a consulting contract to a consulting company that happens to be in another state; if employer company is also in the tax free state than they are giving contract in the same state. Make sure that the documents reflect income in the tax free state; otherwise you will still end-up paying state taxes.

Now, you are the CEO of a consulting company in a tax-free state. You know what to do – if you have forgotten, please review chapter 2 again. Key items being (i) don't draw large salary; (ii) properly structure operating expenses of your consulting company; (iii) leave income in your consulting company; and (iv) consulting company can contribute into your retirement, buy health/life/auto insurances or anything else that is required for its employee, the CEO.

Your job is gone. You are now a business owner, you run your business by the law and pay zero taxes – it is not absolute zero, every year you need to pay a tiny amount as business registration fee – for the C Corporation.[5]

Your personal taxes have been eliminated: your salary or income is at the poverty line, you don't pay federal taxes. You are residing in a tax free state; state tax is not an issue.

Your consulting company is in a tax free state; again, state tax is not an issue. Federal taxes on the income of consulting company are still an issue? Is it really?

---

[5] *It is state's business registration fee (filing of articles of incorporation); it varies from state to state, it will be on the order of $150; filing of list of officers will also require similar fee.*

From its income (that was equivalent to your salary, when you were an employee), consulting company has paid a small salary and a large amount in operating expenses – explained in chapter 2. It is pre-tax dollars, so you get more buying power to begin with. The cost of insurances and retirement is also operating expenses; after subtraction, income to the consulting company should be same as employee salary. The rent of the room/studio is also an operating expense; again, you are paying it with pre-tax dollars. The left over, if there is left over, should not be much. If for some reason, you have goofed in structuring of operating expenses and left over amount is $15,000-$20,000; hire an administrative assistant or a receptionist or a VP of operation or whatever position you deem suitable for the consulting company. It can be your spouse, kids, parents or anyone else with whom you don't mind sharing. Consulting company will need to pay a small amount in FICA taxes for its employees, but you can live with it when there are no other taxes.

We Are Unemployed

In chapter 1, I mentioned the tabooed word "poor"; the word "unemployed" is similarly tabooed. You need to get out of that psychological hurdle. Lot of people call themselves "self employed"; it is hurting you. Just by calling self-employed, you increase your taxes; now, you also have to pay employer's FICA taxes. Be proud to be unemployed. If you really have problem, call yourself "retired". There are plenty of rich people in their 30s and 40s who are retired, they don't call themselves self-employed, why are you?

You are unemployed and can't find a job, find a disaster, anywhere in the world. Setup a relief fund, advertise online and rack-up donations. Besides salary and operating expenses, now you can also have a vacation in that exotic land. Just take few pictures of victims in case someone asks questions. When your funds start to run low, find another disaster and setup another relief fund. You need not to look for a job; you are home free.

Small business owners, farmers and ranchers after ditching self proprietary structure and establishing a C Corporation should become unemployed periodically: CEO being fired, your kid becomes the CEO; couple of years later, the kid CEO is fired and you take back the position of the CEO. During your unemployed year (or two), get unemployment benefits – C Corporation is paying taxes, get some benefits whatever you can; at-least for lifetime allowable limit of five years.

While you are unemployed, transfer your retirement savings (401k and IRA), contribution C Corporation made, into the Roth IRA without paying taxes as described in the example of chapter 1.

People who lost their jobs and can't find one, many who have stopped looking, I am sorry for your suffering; don't rely on the government or big corporations. Start a new career in non profit organization.

A number of people either thinking or enrolling in school, hoping a high-school, college degree or even MS will lend them a job. Before you enroll in a university and giveaway thousands of dollars, make sure that your assumption is correct that you will get a job after the graduation. I have taught in engineering colleges, more than half of the curriculum wasn't of any relevance. For example, at San Jose State Electrical Engineering Department, Solid State Physics was a **mandatory course** for all MS students – there may be one or two jobs for Solid State Physicist, for that there are plenty of people with Ph. D. degrees. Who's gonna hire a fresh graduate, not even in Silicon Valley. Semiconductor physicist's jobs are gone to the South-East Asia 10-15 years ago. Make sure you will get relevant education.

By now you know that you are on your own; you need to start your own business. If you are poor and broke but by enrolling to a school allow you to take large student loan, then enroll and take the maximum possible amount in the student loan. Enroll in the program to begin but start a non-profit business from that money, do charity and become a saint for the rest of your life.

Student Loan

Lot of people will have difficulty in digesting what I am proposing, it defies all conventional wisdom – you can't play and expect to win a rigged game by conventional wisdom. So, read it; sleep and think it over and then read it again. You are still in school, you have time to take tactical action, but you need to establish strategy now.

Instead of thinking minimum amount to borrow as student loan, borrow maximum; it is their money, you can take it under student loan, rack it up. Instead of $20,000, take $200,000 if you can. Don't let your parents spend their retirement savings or take a second mortgage; take a student loan, take two, take three. It will become impossible to pay back, so don't pay back, not a dime. With accumulating interest, amount will keep increasing, let it be. The only thing you need to make sure is that you don't have any income in your name – no earning and no assets, live poor and broke the whole life. Did I mention earlier that "poor" and "broke" are just words? Also, let me repeat what I mentioned earlier, not owning doesn't mean that you cannot be beneficiary of that asset. When your benefactor has control over the asset, you can do whatever you want with that asset; but when it is not in your name or in your control, other person cannot take it away from you.

A word of caution, don't let your parent's assets become collateral; otherwise, they will come after your parents. This is yet another reason for parents to shift their assets under an abstract entity, i.e. a trust. I think non-profit umbrella is a much better choice – charity for the poor male Libra, born in Toledo and have tattoo of the name of charity founder on his left arm.

When you don't have earnings and assets, they can't take anything from you, neither can they collect student loan whatever amount it may be. That is why, rack it up, you are not paying it back, ever. Learn from celebrities, they rack-up debt, go "broke" and live luxurious life.

I mentioned to establish strategy now. This includes a number of things to avoid, earnings and assets in your name is just one. For example, you need to educate your parents that they should not give you any inheritance; instead they should put it in a trust and name you a beneficiary but not its trustee. Many of your parents may find it a bit confusing. Hence, just to be sure, I will describe it in the next section. Protection of inheritance is important, particularly when you know that creditors (banks who gave student loan) will come after you; don't mess it up.

If loan is not paid, it will be deducted from social security when you retire. When you won't have any earning in your whole life, you will not be paying social security taxes. In most likelihood, social security will be bankrupt much before you will even qualify. Social security is the biggest Ponzi scheme ever designed – take money from new members and give it to the older members; as long as there are new members, pyramid continues. It is a Ponzi scheme because payments are not based upon need, simply based upon age – does a billionaire really need social security? When the next generation, you, won't pay, the lack of new members will make this pyramid collapse.

But let say it continues: (a) when you won't pay FICA taxes, you won't have enough credits to get much social security; (b) they have already shifted full retirement age to 67; by the time, you will be 67, the full retirement age will be in late 70s or even 80s; (c) in the best of circumstances, if you get few dollars from social security that go towards your student loan, let it go, it is just peanuts.

There are two major strategic steps you have to take: (i) do not have any earning in your name the whole life. It will take some work and constant vigilance; (ii) there should be no assets in your name; you can be a beneficiary but not a controlling party, i.e. a trustee.

These are your trumps, don't waste them; if played correctly, you can take their money and they can't do anything.

If your parents have already set-up a non-profit organization for themselves as I suggested earlier; after graduation, become life-long volunteer for that charitable cause. If they didn't do it, you do it; charity is good for your soul, body, money, taxes and loan.

If your parents are farmers and they set-up a church/temple, become its care-taker. Serve god for the rest of your life, god will be pleased and won't let anyone bothering you for paying back the loan.

If your parents established a C Corporation and pass it to you by assigning you the CEO and director; don't draw any salary. In chapter 2, I did write that taking $1 in salary is good PR; in your case, it would also be a good fiscal choice.

If you do take a job, work as an employee of a C Corporation, consulting company; again, don't take salary from the consulting company.

When you won't pay, what they are going to do; you are "poor" and "broke". Yes, it is against the conventional wisdom, but at-least now you can play the game. Your parents didn't like to be called nerd or geek; they also don't like to be poor and broke. You like to be nerd and geek, and you will love to be poor and broke.

Take student loans in your personal name, as much as you can, take it even if you don't need it (banks did, why not you), but keep all your earnings when you start working under an abstract name – a C Corporation, or a charity, or even a church. They took your parent's money, their livelihood, their homes, your home; get even. Take their money and never give it back – your parents couldn't do anything, you can. They are mortgaging your future, the whole working life; take every possible loan you can and pay the loan back in future, in the after-life.

Asset Protection Trusts

A number of states, Nevada, Alaska, Wyoming, Hawaii, South Dakota, Delaware, Missouri, Utah, Oklahoma, Tennessee, New Hampshire, Rhode Island and Virginia (effective July 2012), allow to form self-settle trust, where the founder (settlor) can be a trustee and a beneficiary. These Asset Protection Trusts (APT) are also known as Domestic APT or with the state prefix, i.e. NAPT for Nevada APT. Before 1997, such trusts were available in the

Caribbean countries and some European nations such as Switzerland; called offshore APT (OAPT) or foreign APT (FAPT).

These APT also have a statue (time varies from state to state) for creditor to make claim; once the time is passed, creditor cannot make claim against the asset. Because of this statue, rich and celebrity often use these trust – when they run-up a debt, creditor cannot claim assets in the APT.

The reasoning of going offshore were: (i) if creditor file suit in that Caribbean Island, they can move to another island and keep frustrating the creditor; (ii) they can ignore the judgment by simply stating that offshore trust doesn't let them bring money back to the United States (impossible to act).

The second reason was shot-down in a classic 1999 case, FTC vs Affordable Media, LLC (case is often referred to Anderson case). State court as well as 9th Circuit Appeals court didn't accept the "impossibility defense"; Anderson couple were held in contempt of court and sent to jail.

In a sense, the court established that the founder/settlor and trustee has control and thus, can be held responsible to pay the awarded judgment.

What it has to do with student loans?

In the previous section, when I mentioned inheritance and strategy, I mentioned to be a beneficiary but not the trustee. Often parents assign their kids as future trustees, basically passing the control of the trust to the kids. Being trustee, kid becomes responsible for his/her creditors. You want to help the kid, don't give control to the kid when kid is racking-up student loan. Help him/her, name him/her beneficiary who will get benefits at the discretion of the trustee; you remain the trustee and the controller. Court cannot hold kid responsible to pay the loan and take away inheritance; effectively, kid never gets the inheritance.

Eventually, you will need to pass the trust, assign your grand children as trustee. When they take student loan, they should relinquish the control to their children or someone else. Person who has student loan should not be named as a controlling party.

Optimization Algorithm

Starting from chapter 1, I have many political statements in this book. So, let me try to give an algorithm for political problems. Please remember, money is catalyst but money doesn't make laws, politicians do. Hence, the root cause is the people in the Washington and state capitols and you, who send them there; yes you!

In each election, media shows a map of the United States in Red and Blue colors for each state. Do you know how ridiculous that is? It means United States is not a democracy; it has two kings – a Red king and a Blue king. You need to re-establish the democracy; remove the Red king and the Blue king from power. As a voter, a large number of people put a label on their forehead of being Democrat or Republican and subsequently, vote for the party man; not for the best man. When you play politics, don't complaint of being the victim of politicians.

When you vote thinking that if I won't vote for my party man, other party man will win; you are voting because of external factor – other party man is an external man, he/she is not in your party. In some sense, you are voting under "external duress".

The biggest intellectual gift of the United States to the world is individualism. Individualism is associated with independent person; vote for independent person, not the party man.

In every election, in every district, there are plenty of independent candidates, some lawyers, doctors, accountants, business men. Vote for them, send them to Washington and state capitols; let independent candidate have the majority and both parties in chaos; kings out.

In Computer Engineering and Computer Science, there is a standard optimization method – when stuck with a poor result, reset all parameters to chaos; when parametric values will settle you will get a better result, possibly an optimized result.[6] This is controlled chaos. In daily life, you call it – rock the boat; rocking the boat breaks down status quo. Getting out of the status quo is necessary and better than the uncontrolled chaos in Washington and at state capitols.

Independents don't have a party affiliation. They don't have money either, that's why they can't run attack ads. They don't have major lobbyist's connections – when they will win without lobbyists, they will do what is good for the constituents.

Yes, this is the basic assumption; we don't know how good/bad this assumption is and we won't know

---

[6] *Such methods are taught in courses on algorithms.*

unless you all vote for independent candidates everywhere.

All these newly elected independents by definition will not be "powerful"; they will be careful in their behavior, what they propose and vote for. Both parties will continue, but whether democrat or republican, won't have "power"; both parties will be restructured and forced to operate differently. Vote along the party line to make a law or amend one will have no meaning, votes of independents will determine what to pass and what to reject.

Please note, I am not suggesting a third party. Third party would mean a third king. Bring individualism to the government – government by the people; independent, common, middle class people; people who don't have "power".

When majority of government is independent, they will form collations to support a proposal based upon its merit. Lobbyist will still be there but independents will be careful working for them. For different proposal, different people will form collations. No more party line. Furthermore, by default, people will need support of other people; there will be lot less bickering and more work done.

Some may argue that majority of independents will not be able to form collation and will create chaos. But you see, that's exactly my point – without creating chaos, public cannot filter and identify the people who really should be governing. Party men are bad; message of independents is poorly heard, so it is hard to judge. Making matter worse, political attack ads by the party men and lobbyists really drown their message; without iteration, selection of right person is close to impossible. After the first election, if government is in complete chaos then in the second follow-up election, public can eliminate elected independents and more party members (who got elected). Algorithm is an iterative process by nature; when parametric values stabilize, you will get a solution.

These repeat elections will cost money, public money, but no where close to trillion dollars! In the end, public will get a government that will really lead and govern the country.

It is election time, this is your chance to get rid of the Red and the Blue Kings; why wait till December, end their world in November.

This algorithm always gives a solution; it is fail proof – I can't see if you are smiling or not, but you are entertained, are you not!

Chapter 6: Summary and Concluding Remarks

Rich pay hardly 15% in taxes and if you bring your taxes to zero, will America go bankrupt? No, house doesn't bankrupt in monopoly. They are playing monopoly; it's paper money – for the government and the wall-street, not for you. US treasury can print any amount, anytime, anywhere. Value of your assets disappears that's your problem; they can even change the inflation accounting parameters, so that it doesn't look bad in the news. There is no collateral and their printing presses are all over the country – Philadelphia, Denver, San Francisco. Wall-street can take any amount, anytime; better yet, treasury will give it to them whether they want it or not. So, wall-street is free to bet. Do you notice that the word "bet" is inherently gambling, there is no other association – free and open gambling and New York doesn't allow gambling, yeah right. Get out of the cocoon of ethics and morality; you cannot play the game from inside the cocoon.

When you will eliminate your taxes, they will print little more paper, no big deal. The only people who need to worry about anything are Chinese, their Trillion dollars go poof! They are on the hook anyway; they can't sell US treasury bills because prices will fall. With US treasury printing; they have to buy more for the same reason. In Electrical Engineering, it is called Positive Feedback; it leads to larger oscillations and eventually smoke coming out of the circuit. Right now, you are seeing oscillations; either get a fire extinguisher or **shut-off the power** before smoke comes out.

Don't try to compete with the rich and the powerful; you neither got wealth, nor power. Competing with them under same conditions is impossible. When faced with an impossible task, change the very fundamental assumption; the task not only become simple, the difficulty disappears. When given an impossible knot to open, Alexander didn't bother to open it; he took his sword and cut it, opening of the knot became meaningless. There are hundreds of such stories; I am just repeating the moral of such stories. They expect you to compete to become rich and powerful; instead, become "poor" and "broke" and change the equation fundamentally – whether it is taxes or student loan, problem becomes meaningless.

Let me try to give an itemized list of what is written in the previous chapters that you may want to consider:

1. The whole premise of this book is that you need to make changes in your life-style. You need to learn the rules of the game and play; you can't stand on the sideline and keep getting hit by other players running in every direction. Shouting from the sideline is just noise and excitement for other watchers sitting in the stadium or in front of TV – other common folks. It doesn't do anything to the game itself; players and coach don't hear the noise, they keep headphones on, to block the noise. Run, play,

running and playing is healthy for you, in more ways than one. Don't listen to President Obama, he will spin it into a political statement; listen to Michelle Obama, she shops at same stores as you do and teaches everyone to play.[7]

2. Get familiar with the city/county/state/federal laws; you may be able to device a better plan. City/county/state laws vary anyway and there are plenty of gottchas. This book or any other book can only provide generalized discussion. Familiarity with the city/county/state laws will not only help you devising a particular strategy, you may even be able to devise better than written in any book.

3. Consult and hire a lawyer, he/she can prepare papers and guide you through. Talk to a number of attorney and also search and read on the Internet before you sign-up with an attorney. Don't be surprised with a number of estate

---

[7] *Comment is with the highest respect and compliment.*

planning attorneys if they didn't know about APTs. The estate planning for many financial planners and attorneys is a holding trust, will, medical directive and power of attorney. After a little bit reading and with a computer program, you can do these things yourself; you will probably save a thousand dollars.

4. Don't become greedy, don't become one of them. In housing debacle, your greed is equally to blame. If you see everybody doing something and you jump-in without educating yourself, that's sheep's behavior – you will end-up in the ditch too. Greed also motivates people to bend or bypass the law and that is how they end-up in jail. Don't break any laws.

5. Students who are drowning in the student loans can turn the tables around. If universities and banks continue to mortgage their working life, they can take the money and never pay back. If student decide not to pay back, the rule of thumb is not to keep anything in your name and

in your control. If something is not in your name and not in your control, it cannot be taken away from you.

6. To reduce and eliminate taxes the base principle is to bring your AGI to under poverty line. This can be achieved by not having large income. A number of actions are required; it creates little paper work but skipping paper work may lead to trouble with the authorities.

7. To eliminate the state taxes, the simplest thing is to move to a state that doesn't have state taxes. Most rich declare a tax-free state as their residence, you should too. The little expense (rental, business registration fee etc.) will pay for itself by eliminating large amount of state taxes.

8. Whether it is a for-profit-corporation or a non-profit-corporation, executives enjoy various expenses under operating expenses; once again, paper work should not be skipped.

9. Self proprietary company is bad structure for asset protection as well as for taxes. All business owners, farmers, ranchers, service providers should think-of using the structure of the C Corporation. Some key benefits of C Corporation are:

   a. Personal protection against liability claims and business debt.

   b. Lower tax rate.

   c. Sale of business can be structured to minimize taxes.

   d. Business can be transferred to heirs by simply appointing them as directors.

10. Keeping income/assets in the name of corporation doesn't hurt when corporation is completely under your control. Corporate tax rate is lower than the personal tax-rate; taking income in personal name triggers higher taxes.

11. Non-profit corporations by default keep surplus income under tax-exempt umbrella and use it to grow business; business grows tax-free. All

small business owner, farmers, ranchers, service providers should consider setting their businesses as non-profit; if anytime money is needed, they can convert it into their name.

12. Before donating to a charity, person should look at the financial statement and tax filing of the charity and determine if the donation will really go to the victim or majority of it will go to the executives/employees of the charity.

13. Pouring more money into schools is not a solution to degrading educational standard. Faculty salaries have steadily increased over 400% since 1972, while educational standard has steadily gone down. Similarly, issuing new bonds for yet another fancy school building is a waste of money; fancy buildings have nothing to do with kid's learning. Parents of K12 kids should look into online schools; these schools offer uniform education that is at global par and at a fraction of the cost.

14. There is too much money in the system; it needs to be taken out. Without the removal of big money, the broken political system cannot be repaired. A forced chaos by voters by eliminating both parties from the power and sending independents to the Washington and the State Capitols may lead to repair.

15. Every religion teaches reasoning. Before you take any action, whether the suggestion is mine or someone else's; think it through and reason it out.

Few final comments: The recent recession has shattered job based dreams for thousands of people. People who have jobs are also anxious because they have been tossed-around, their salaries and benefits are cut and work demand has increased. They are living in a constant fear of the pink-slip. Today, people need to re-think of their own welfare and livelihood. They need to take control of their work and career – enough with that stupid boss and stingy company. By starting a business, regardless of age, education and background, person steps into the realms of independence; person creates job for himself/herself, job that is under his own control. Job for one's own self – that's independence, freedom. In principle, many people imagine such freedom but don't take action because of the fear of unknown.

Family and friends, the nay-sayers, make the matter worse by citing the lack of experience and often myopically discourage to venture into entrepreneurship. In my opinion, for a large number of jobs, beyond a certain stage, experience is in-fact a negative. It often restricts brain, handicapping person's imagination in visualization of something new; thus, psychology prevents person to get out of the comfort-zone. A 10-years veteran "experienced" person means that the person has been doing the same thing over and over for the past 10-years. Most likely this person will be resistive to new tools and the mode of operation that requires change in the work style of the past 10-years. Keep doing the exact same thing over and over again, it becomes boring, even sex!

Learning by self mistakes is the "hard-way". This "hard-learning" is often seen in the stock market when people trade stocks/options without doing proper research or without educating themselves on the risk.

The "easy-way" to learn is by educating oneself and from the mistakes of others. This easy learning doesn't give working experience to a person. Is working experience really needed? Who would you like to work with – a person who doesn't make mistakes because he/she already knows pit-falls by observing others and does everything right the first time; or with the person who constantly make mistakes and cannot do anything right if he/she has not experienced it before. I would like to point-out that "easy learning" doesn't come easily, it requires continuous and extensive reading, observation of the work of others and constant objective evaluation of the self-work.

There is first time for everything. Fear based upon inexperience should not be a deterring factor. Similarly, fear of failure is inexcusable; not trying means you have already failed. After trying-out certain class of ideas and business, regardless of the success or failure, it is highly likely that you will become independent. If successful, then indeed you can buy that apartment on the Fifth Avenue in lower Manhattan with an Austin Martin: *you will never know until you try it out*.

□ □ □